Assessing and Teaching Reading Comprehension and Pre-Writing K-3

Volume 1

K. Michael Hibbard
Elizabeth A. Wagner

EYE ON EDUCATION
6 DEPOT WAY WEST, SUITE 106
LARCHMONT, NY 10538
(914) 833–0551
(914) 833–0761 fax
www.eyeoneducation.com

Library of Congress Cataloging-in-Publication Data

Hibbard, K. Michael.
Assessing and teaching reading comprehension and pre-writing, K-3 / K. Michael Hibbard, Elizabeth A. Wagner.
    p cm.
Includes bibliographical references.
ISBN 1-930556-42-X
1. Language arts (EArly childhood)--Ability testing. 2. Reading comprehension. I. Wagner, Elizabeth A., 1950- II. Title.

LB1139.5.L35 H53 2003
372.6049--dc21   2002072166

10 9 8 7 6 5 4 3 2 1

Editorial and production services provided by
Richard H. Adin Freelance Editorial Services
52 Oakwood Blvd., Poughkeepsie, NY 12603-4112
(845-471-3566)

Also Available from EYE ON EDUCATION

Assessing and Teaching
Reading Comprehension and Writing K-3, Volume 2
by K. Michael Hibbard and Elizabeth A. Wagner

Beyond Stories:
Young Children's Nonfiction Composition
by Susan Britsch

Reading, Writing, and Gender:
Instructional Strategies and Classroom Activities
That Work for Girls and Boys
by Gail Goldberg and Barbara Roswell

Teaching, Learning and Assessment Together:
The Reflective Classroom
by Arthur K. Ellis

Technology Tools for Young Learners
by Leni von Blanckensee

Buddies:
Reading Writing and Math Lessons
by Pia Hansen Powell

Better Instruction Through Assessment:
What Your Students Are Trying to Tell You
by Leslie Walker Wilson

Assessment Portfolios for Elementary Students
Milwaukee Public Schools

Open-Ended Questions in Elementary Mathematics:
Instruction and Assessment
by Mary Kay Dyer and Christine Moynihan

A Collection of Performance Tasks and Rubrics
Primary School Mathematics
by Charlotte Danielson and Pia Hansen

A Collection of Performance Tasks and Rubrics
Upper Elementary School Mathematics
by Charlotte Danielson

Mathematics the Write Way:
Activities for Every Elementary Classroom
by Marilyn S. Neil

Teacher Retention
What is Your Weakest Link?
by India J. Podsen

Coaching and Mentoring First-Year and Student Teachers
by India J. Podsen and Vicki M. Denmark

Handbook on Teacher Portfolios
for Evaluation and Professional Development
by Pamela D. Tucker, James H. Stronge,
and Christopher R. Gareis

The School Portfolio Toolkit
A Planning, Implementation, and Evaluation Guide
for Continuous School Improvement
by Victoria L. Bernhardt

Data Analysis for Comprehensive Schoolwide Improvement
by Victoria L. Bernhardt

Navigating Comprehensive School Change:
A Guide for the Perplexed
by Thomas G. Chenoweth and Robert B. Everhart

Dealing With Difficult Teachers, 2d ed.
by Todd Whitaker

Motivating and Inspiring Teachers:
The Educational Leader's Guide for Building Staff Morale
by Todd Whitaker, Beth Whitaker, and Dale Lumpa

Teaching Matters
Motivating & Inspiring Yourself
by Todd and Beth Whitaker

Feeling Great! The Educator's Guide for
Eating Better, Exercising Smarter, and Feeling Your Best
by Todd Whitaker& Jason Winkle

What Great Principals Do Differently:
Fifteen Things That Matter Most
by Todd Whitaker

Dealing With Difficult Parents
(And With Parents in Difficult Situations)
by Todd Whitaker and Douglas J. Fiore

Bouncing Back!
How Your School Can Succeed in the Face of Adversity
by Jerry Patterson, Janice Patterson, & Loucrecia Collins

Table of Contents

1

A Roadmap to This Book

Topics In This Chapter

♦ An overview of this book.
♦ Explanation of how the Standards for the Assessment of Reading and Writing by the National Council of Teachers of English and the International Reading Association are carried out by the strategies presented in this book.

A Graphic Overview of This Book

Figure 1.1 presents a graphic that highlights the contents of this book. Students use thinking skills and reading comprehension strategies to interact with texts, and to connect those texts to other texts and to personal experiences. They reveal their comprehension through speaking, drawing, graphic organizers, and writing. This book focuses on the pre-writing activities of speaking, drawing, and graphic organizers. The second book in this two-book series titled, *Assessing and Teaching Reading Comprehension and Writing, K–3*, builds on the pre-writing strategies in this book.

Authentic performance tasks are created to engage students with fiction and nonfiction texts and use thinking skills such as sequencing, listing, describing, categorizing, inferring, predicting, comparing, contrasting, judging and evaluating. The performance tasks ask the students to discuss what they have learned; draw and label pictures; and put information into a wide range of graphic organizers.

Assessment tools including assessment lists, analytic rubrics, and holistic rubrics are used to assess and evaluate this type of student work.

Figure 1.1 shows that following classroom routines, following directions, working cooperatively with others, and self-assessment create a foundation for the improvement of language arts skills. Self-assessment is an essential part of the strategies presented in this book and is introduced through helping students improve their behavior in the classroom.

Figure 1.1. Revealing Reading Comprehension through Speaking, Drawing, Graphic Organizers, and Writing

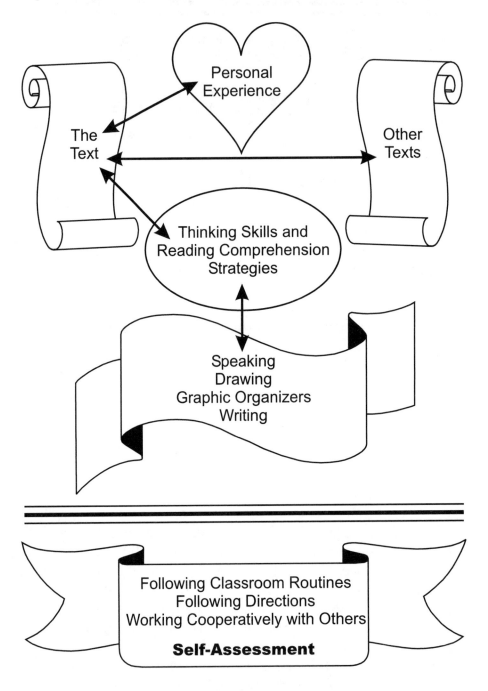

The Topics for Each Chapter
Figure 1.2 presents the topics for each chapter.

Figure 1.2. Topics for Each Chapter

Chapter Number	Chapter Title	Topics
1	A Roadmap to This Book	• An overview of this book. • Explanation of how the Standards for the Assessment of Reading and Writing by the National Council of Teachers of English and the International Reading Association are carried out by the strategies presented in this book.
2	Assessing Classroom Behavior, Work Habits, and Cooperative Group Learning Skills	• Strategies to engage students in learning about the specific behaviors they should exhibit in the classroom. • Strategies to engage students in self-assessment so they learn to take more responsibility for their performance and improve their behavior.
3	Assessing Comprehension through Teacher-Lead Discussions in Various Types of Reading Groups	• Strategies to create questions based on a framework for reading comprehension for use during various reading group activities. • Strategies to create tools to assess and evaluate reading comprehension exhibited by students during reading group activities.
4	Assessing Comprehension of Fiction through Drawing	• Strategies for using a framework for reading comprehension that focuses on thinking-skill verbs to make performance tasks for fiction, asking students to draw and present orally. • Strategies to make analytic rubrics and assessment lists for judging the quality of drawings and oral presentations. • Strategies to use performance tasks and assessment tools in the context of language arts lessons.

5	Assessing Comprehension of Nonfiction through Drawing	• Strategies for using a framework for reading comprehension that focuses on thinking-skill verbs to make performance tasks for nonfiction which asks students to draw and present orally. • Strategies to make analytic rubrics and assessment lists for judging the quality of drawings and oral presentations. • Strategies to use performance tasks and assessment tools in the context of language arts lessons.
6	Assessing Comprehension through the Use of Graphic Organizers	• Strategies for using graphic organizers to help students process information according to the thinking-skill verb used in the task. • Strategies to create performance tasks that use graphic organizers and oral presentation. • Strategies to create assessment tools to assess the quality of a student's use of graphic organizers.

Organization of Each Chapter

Each chapter begins with a list of the topics covered in that chapter. Performance tasks and assessment tools, including assessment lists, analytic rubrics, and holistic rubrics, are included. A list of the books on which the performance tasks are based is at the end of the chapter, as is a glossary of terms.

Standards for the Assessment of Reading and Writing

The summary of the standards from the book titled, *Standards for the Assessment of Reading and Writing*, 1994, International Reading Association and the National Council of Teachers of English, ISBN 0-87207-674-1, and the description of the connections between them and the materials and strategies presented in this book follow.

Standard 1: The Interests of the Student Are Paramount in Assessment

Summary of Standard 1	*Connection between the Standard and the Materials and Strategies of This Book*
The purpose of assessment is to improve student performance. The very process of assessing reading comprehension and writing should make the student a better reader and writer. Reading and writing are used to find and communicate information, ideas, and feelings. Assessment should be authentic and focus on how well students use reading and writing to learn and communicate. Finally, because the assessment process includes opportunities for the student to assess and evaluate the quality of their work, the assessment process helps the student become a reflective learner.	The performance tasks presented in this book are authentic opportunities for students to use reading and writing for learning and communication. Each performance task is built around thinking-skill verbs and components of the writing process. The assessment lists are derived from rubrics related to speaking, drawing, using graphic organizers, and writing. The performance tasks are embedded in units of instruction to serve as learning activities and opportunities to assess student performance. Each performance task has an assessment list that is used before, during, and after a performance task to assess the quality of a student's work.

Standard 2: The Primary Purpose of Assessment Is to Improve Teaching and Learning

Summary of Standard 2	*Connection between the Standard and the Materials and Strategies of This Book*
The interests of the student are served if teaching and learning improves. This standard emphasizes the importance of reflection by both the student and the teacher. Through self-reflection, the learner identifies strengths and weaknesses and then sets and carries out goals to improve their own performance. Likewise, through self-reflection, the teacher identifies strengths and weaknesses of the materials and strategies of teaching and works to improve both. The assessment process must foster this self-reflection and improvement on the part of both student and teacher.	Self-assessment helps students learn to pay attention and take responsibility for the quality of their work. Analytic and holistic rubrics are also provided in this book for drawing, speaking, and using graphic organizers. These assessment tools provide another source of information for teachers to use to gain information about student performance. Teachers assess the students' work and the quality of their self-assessment through the use of assessment lists and rubrics. The information from using assessment lists and rubrics becomes the basis for plans to improve instruction.

Standard 3: Assessment Must Reflect and Enable Critical Inquiry into Curriculum and Instruction

Summary of Standard 3	Connection between the Standard and the Materials and Strategies of This Book
Because reading and writing are complex acts used in very flexible ways, curriculum should plan for the use of reading and writing for these authentic purposes. The curriculum must also include assessments that are well-suited to authentic purposes of reading and writing. Analysis and reflection on the data from assessments helps the teacher decide if the curriculum and assessments are encouraging the use of reading and writing as authentic tools for learning.	Each performance task is an authentic use of reading and writing for the purposes of learning and communicating. Each performance task asks the student to produce a product for a specific audience. Students are learning that reading and writing serves to answer their own questions and also to teach, inform, or entertain an audience. Teachers evaluate the success of performance tasks as authentic opportunities to use reading and writing.

Standard 4: Assessment Must Recognize and Reflect the Intellectually And Socially Complex Nature of Reading and Writing and the Important Roles of School, Home, and Society in Literacy Development

Summary of Standard 4	Connection between the Standard and the Materials and Strategies of This Book
Reading and writing are such complex acts that no one type of assessment is sufficient. Therefore, a set of carefully chosen assessments should be used. These assessments must include opportunities for students to show how well they can use reading and writing for authentic learning and communication. In addition, data from these assessments should not be reduced to a single rating or score.	• Performance tasks should be one component in a language literacy assessment plan. Teachers and administrators should work together to use a set of assessments that helps the classroom teacher make decisions to improve instruction. • The assessment lists and analytic rubrics used in this book provide information about the specific strengths and weaknesses of each student.

Standard 5: Assessment Must Be Fair and Equitable

Summary of Standard 5	Connection between the Standard and the Materials and Strategies of This Book
Assessments must be free of cultural bias and students must have a reasonable opportunity to learn what is to be assessed.	• Performance tasks and assessment tools are created and modified by teachers to be fair and equitable to students. • Teachers select a performance task to use and then plan instruction to help students learn what the performance task will ask them to do. Therefore the students will have many opportunities to learn the content of what will be assessed.

Standard 6: The Consequences of an Assessment Procedure Are the First, and the Most Important, Consideration in Establishing the Validity of the Assessment

Summary of Standard 6	Connection between the Standard and the Materials and Strategies of This Book
Assessment must help to improve student performance in the authentic use of reading and writing for learning and communication. A set of assessments would include both tests for specific skills and assessments of how well students read and write to learn and communicate. Including performance assessments in the assessment plan will encourage teachers to use reading and writing in the classroom for authentic purposes. Assessments should help classroom teachers make day-to-day decisions that help adjust and differentiate their materials and strategies to improve the performance of all students. The amount of time spent in assessment must be balanced with the time spent using data from the assessment to drive further instruction.	Performance tasks and assessment tools are one component of instruction in balance with other classroom activities. The assessment lists provide an efficient way for the teacher to communicate expectations to students and to assess their performance. The performance tasks are worth the time they take. Performance tasks ask students to use knowledge and language arts skills in the context of constructing thoughts and communicating them to others. Classroom instruction that precedes the performance tasks focus both on specific skills and how to use them to solve real learning and communication problems.

Standard 7: The Teacher Is the Most Important Agent of Assessment

Summary of Standard 7	Connection between the Standard and the Materials and Strategies of This Book
First and foremost, teachers should be readers and writers. They should continuously improve their knowledge of the research and best practices of reading and writing. Some of the best professional development occurs when teachers discuss and share judgments about student work and plan materials and strategies to improve student performance.	• Conversations about student work, as discussed through the lens of assessment lists and rubrics is excellent professional development. Based on what they learn, teachers plan improvements in performance tasks and their supporting materials. • Teachers learn more about the content and process skills in their disciplines when they collaborate to design and modify existing performance tasks and assessment lists and create new performance tasks and assessment lists.

Standard 8: The Assessment Process Should Involve Multiple Perspectives and Sources of Data

Summary of Standard 5	Connection between the Standard and the Materials and Strategies of This Book
A variety of assessments must be used to take a comprehensive look at student performance. Anecdotal Records, Running Records with Retelling, High Frequency Words, Letter Name Inventory, Letter Sound Inventory, Developmental Spelling, Dictation, the Gates MacGinitie Reading Test, and Performance Tasks as presented in this book are examples of assessments to consider. There should be a balance between assessment of skill and assessments of authentic use of reading and writing for learning and communication.	Performance tasks are only one component of a balanced assessment plan. They are used in balance with other types of tests and assessments to get a comprehensive view of reading.

Standard 9: Assessment Must Be Based in the School Community

Summary of Standard 9	*Connection between the Standard and the Materials and Strategies of This Book*
It is important for educators, parents, and other members of the community to talk with one another to understand and communicate how reading and writing are rich, complex, flexible tools people use to learn and communicate. The school's curriculum, instructional practices, and assessments all work together to reflect an understanding of reading and writing. This common understanding will help a partnership flourish among educators, parents, and other community members.	Performance tasks and assessment lists are excellent ways to show parents how reading and writing are tools for learning. Student work accompanied by an assessment list that has been used by the student for self-assessment and by the teacher to assess the quality of the self-assessment and the student work is valued by parents. Performance tasks, assessment lists, and student work are excellent materials for parent conferences.

Standard 10: All Members of the Educational Community—Students, Parents, Teachers, Administrators, Policy Makers, and the Public—Must Have a Voice in the Development, Interpretation and Reporting of Assessment

Summary of Standard 10	*Connection between the Standard and the Materials and Strategies of This Book*
Educators, parents, and other members of the educational community engage in a dialogue that reflects and defines the understanding of how the data will be communicated to the public. The outcome of this process is that parents are well-informed about their children's performance in reading and writing and are happy with the work that teachers are doing to improve performance.	The use of performance tasks and assessment lists as one component of teaching and assessment must be explained to the Board of Education, parents, and others. The authentic nature of performance tasks makes them very appealing to all concerned audiences. It is important to show how data on student performance is generated from performance tasks and how it is used to drive instruction. Finally, it is important to show improvements in student performance over time.

Standard 11: Parents Must Be Involved As Active, Essential Participants in the Assessment Process

Summary of Standard 11	Connection between the Standard and the Materials and Strategies of This Book
Schools need to reach out to parents in a wide variety of ways that respond to the diverse needs and life commitments of the families. Reporting procedures such as report cards, parent conferences, portfolios, and letters from the school accompanying state test data reports should be planned in collaboration with parents. Parents should also be encouraged to participate in professional development offerings.	Performance tasks and student work can become a central part of parent conferences and other parent meetings. Performance tasks and assessment lists are easy ways to teach parents about what is important in teaching and learning.

2

Teaching and Assessing Classroom Behavior, Work Habits, and Cooperative Group Learning Skills

Topics In This Chapter

♦ Strategies to engage students in learning about the specific behaviors they should exhibit in the classroom

♦ Strategies to engage students in self-assessment so they learn to take more responsibility for their behavior and academic performance.

Begin the Acts of Self-Reflection and Self-Regulation through Focusing on Student Behaviors in the Classroom

Classroom management is an important foundation for learning activities throughout the year. Carrying out classroom routines; working with partners, small groups and the class as a whole group; and students' personal work habits and study skills are challenges for the teacher as well as the students. When these behaviors are constructive, lessons run more smoothly. But when these behaviors are below standard, teaching and learning are both compromised.

Performance assessment is easily introduced in the context of specific behaviors important to a smoothly running classroom, productive group work, and effective personal work habits. Because these behaviors occur every day, the students have concrete experience with them. student performance in these areas can usually be improved through the strategies of self-assessment and self-regulation. Students can experience success and learn to value the use of assessment lists and the strategies of performance-based learning and assessment.

This chapter shows how to use performance-based learning and assessment to improve classroom management and student behavior. This work should be done at the beginning of the school year to foster independence on the part of students so the teacher can focus more time on academics.

A Sequence of Steps to Use Performance Assessment to Improve Student Performance

The following list presents one sequence of steps a teacher could use to improve student performance:

- ◆ Select a type of behavior, skill, or work to assess and improve.
- ◆ Identify the specifics of that type of behavior, skill, or work.
- ◆ Create an analytic rubric to further describe the behavior, skill, or work.
- ◆ Create an assessment list to use as a tool directly with students.
- ◆ Get models or examples of actual student performance and work that shows the level of performance expected from them.
- ◆ Teach students skills and behaviors.
- ◆ Teach students to use assessment lists.
- ◆ Teach students to use models of excellent work as targets or goals.
- ◆ Teach students to set goals to improve their own performance.
- ◆ Repeat these steps.

The following are three categories of skills and a list of behaviors for each:

1. Classroom Skills to Assess, Including:
    - • Following routines
    - • Keeping hands and feet to one's self
    - • Controlling impulsivity
    - • Showing respect and courtesy
    - • Using good personal hygiene

2. Study Skills and Work Habits to Assess, Including:
    - • Following directions for a task
    - • Sticking to the task
    - • Working independently (when you should be working independently)
    - • Working quietly
    - • Being prepared
    - • Being organized
    - • Being neat
    - • Getting work done on time
    - • Printing your name on your work

3. Group (Pairs to Whole Class) Learning Skills to Assess, Including:
    - • Listening

- Taking turns
- Sharing
- Contributing
- Encouraging the participation of others
- Checking for understanding
- Checking directions
- Getting work done on time
- Managing materials and cleaning up

Use "T" Charts to Identify Specific, Observable Behaviors to Assess

A "T" Chart is a type of graphic organizer designed to help identify specific, observable behaviors that are related to a general behavior such as following classroom routines, following directions on a task, or encouraging a friend to participate in a group project.

The three "T" Charts in this chapter show the final products of classroom discussions held by the teacher with students. Figures 2.1, 2.2, and 2.3 show "T" Charts resulting from classroom discussions about the behaviors listed on the top of each. Each "T" Chart may take several discussions over a few days to complete. *The words in italics* are what the teacher scribed onto the chart from discussions with students.

After the teacher talks about the general behavior or skill, such as following classroom routines, he or she then asks the students to imagine what it would "look like" if a student followed the classroom routines. Students take turns suggesting "looks like" statements. The teacher asks follow-up questions to focus these "looks like" statements. For example, a student may say, "I pay attention to the teacher." The teacher may then ask, "What does it look like when you are paying attention to me? What are you doing that tells me that you are paying attention to me?" The student then may reply, "I look at you when you give the Stop-Look-Listen signal." That specific, observable behavior is written in the "looks like" column of the "T" Chart.

After a few items are written in the "looks like" column, the teacher and students then turn their attention to the "sounds like" column and continue the discussion. During the first session, the class may only find a few items for each column. It may take more experience with, and thinking about, following classroom routines to add more items to the "T" Chart. Completed "T" Charts can be displayed in the classroom.

Note: The "T" Chart in Figure 2.1 shows the items selected to be Sure Things, "ST," and the items selected to be a Challenge, "C." The assessment list in Figure 2.7 was constructed based on the use of the "T" Chart in Figure 2.1.

Figure 2.1. Behaviors Important to Following Classroom Routines

When I follow the classroom routines

	it looks like:		*it sounds like:*
ST	I look up when I hear the "Stop, Look, and Listen" signal from my teacher.		I am silent as soon as I hear the "Stop, Look, and Listen" signal from my teacher.
	I am in the center I should be in.	C	I am quiet when I move to a new activity.
	I am in my reading group.	ST	I am using my "quiet sharing voice" when I am in a center with a friend.
	I am writing in my journal.	ST	I use a "whisper voice" when I am thinking out loud.
	I get my own materials and I put them back where they belong.		I am using my "reading group voice" when I am talking in my group
	I know where to go when my work is done.		I use my "strong sharing voice" when I am sharing with the whole class.

Figure 2.2. Behaviors Important to Following Directions for a Task

When I follow directions

it looks like:	*it sounds like:*
I look at the teacher when directions are given.	Only the teacher is talking when the teacher gives directions.
My mouth is not moving when directions are given.	I ask or answer a question when the teacher calls on me.
I raise my hand if I have a question.	My question is about the directions.
My hands and my feet are where they should be.	I use my "quiet whisper voice" when I am thinking out loud about the directions.
I have the materials on my desk that should be there.	I use my "quiet whisper voice" when I ask a friend for help with the directions.
I go to where the materials that I need are in the room.	
I think about what I am supposed to do.	
If I am not sure what to do I ask three friends.	
If I still need help, I go to the teacher.	

Figure 2.3. Behaviors Important to Encouraging Participation

When I encourage my friend to participate

it looks like:	*it sounds like:*
I look at my friend.	I ask my friend a question about the topic.
I smile at my friend.	Only my friend's voice is heard when my friend is talking.
My mouth is not moving when my friend is sharing.	I use my "good manners" by saying please and thank you to my friend.
My hands and feet are to myself.	
I do not touch the things my friend is using.	

Creating Analytic Rubrics

Working on a "T" Chart helps the teacher think about the details of specific behaviors or skills important to a more general behavior. Those details are captured in the "T" Chart. An analytic rubric based on the "T" chart can then be created. Figures 2.4, 2.5, and 2.6 show analytic rubrics for the three corresponding "T" Charts in Figures 2.1, 2.3, and 2.4

To create the analytic rubric for following classroom routines, the teacher made a list of the types of behaviors or skills important to following classroom procedures. Then the teacher put those statements into the left column of the analytic rubric, labeled "Specific Behavior."

Next the teacher wrote specific descriptions for each of the three levels of performance relevant to that specific behavior. The teacher describes what it is like when a student is "Terrific" at paying attention, what a student is like when he or she is only "Okay" at paying attention, and what behavior is like that "Needs Work." Note that the title for the lowest category of performance is not a negative statement such as, "Poor Performance." It is stated, "Needs Work" and means "this behavior needs work and we can do it."

Using Analytic Rubrics

Analytic rubrics are tools that teachers make and use themselves. Sometimes teachers at the same or similar grade levels collaborate to create a rubric so that they all have a common understanding of the levels of quality of the specific behaviors important to a general behavior, such as following classroom routines.

An individual teacher or a team can use the analytic rubric to identify the strengths and needs of students and then plan to adjust and differentiate instruction to improve student performance. Using the same analytic rubric over the course of the year or several years helps the teacher or team see and describe "progress over time" in student behavior. This kind of data can be useful in setting classroom or school improvement objectives and assessing the degree to which the objectives are met.

Students in the primary grades usually do not see or use the whole analytic rubrics directly. The teacher may present one specific behavior such as "Pays attention to the teacher" and the descriptions of the three levels of performance—"Terrific," "Okay," and "Needs Work." The students may then talk about their behavior and decide what their performance has been like. If their behavior is less than "Terrific," they can set goals and plan to improve.

Note: The analytic rubric shown in Figures 2.4 has been marked to show a student's performance on each element in the analytic rubric. This analysis of students' strengths and needs can also be use to construct the assessment list in Figure 2.7.

Figure 2.4. Analytic Rubric for Following Classroom Routines

Specific Behavior	Levels of Performance		
	3: Terrific	2: Okay	1: Needs Work
Pays attention to the teacher.	Stops immediately, is quiet, and looks at the teacher as soon as the Stop-Look-Listen signal is given.	Becomes quiet immediately but may not completely stop work and/or may not look at the teacher.	Does not become quiet, or stop work, or look at the teacher.
Goes to the correct location.	Goes to the correct location immediately, quietly, whenever necessary.	Goes to the correct location immediately, but is not quiet.	Does not go to the correct location, and/or continues to talk and distract others.
Uses the correct voice volume.	Uses the whisper voice, the quiet sharing voice, the reading group voice, and the strong sharing voice in the appropriate settings.	Uses the various voice levels correctly most of the time.	Usually does not use the appropriate voice level.
Uses the correct materials.	Uses the correct materials all the time.	Usually uses the correct materials.	Often does not use the correct materials.
Engages in the correct task.	Is always engaged in the correct task.	Is usually engaged in the correct task.	Often is engaged in the incorrect task.
Controls own behavior.	Always controls own behavior.	Usually controls own behavior.	Often has difficulty controlling own behavior.

Figure 2.5. Analytic Rubric for Following Directions for a Task

Specific Behavior	Levels of Performance		
	3: Terrific	2: Okay	1: Needs Work
Pays attention to the teacher.	Stops immediately, is quiet, and looks at the teacher as soon as the Stop-Look-Listen signal is given.	Becomes quiet immediately but may not completely stop work and/or may not look at the teacher.	Does not become quiet, or stop work, or look at the teacher.
Thinks about the directions.	Always uses Thinking-Out-Loud voice to repeat directions and looks at the examples or models of work to be done.	Usually uses Thinking-Out-Loud voice to repeat directions and looks at the examples or models of work to be done.	Seldom uses Thinking-Out-Loud voice to repeat directions and looks at the examples or models of work to be done.
Gets help when necessary.	The student tried to understand, but realizes that help is needed. The student first looks at the model. Then the student asks three other students for help, and, if that does not work, asks the teacher if necessary.	The student tried to understand, but realizes that help is needed. Then the student goes directly to the teacher without asking other students first.	Goes to the teacher right away for help without trying any other strategies first.
Gets and uses correct materials.	Always goes to the correct place to get materials and then uses them correctly.	Usually knows the correct place to get materials and then usually uses them correctly.	Often does not know the correct place to get materials and then often uses them incorrectly.
Persists on the task.	Always persists.	Usually persists.	Seldom persists.
Controls own behavior.	Always controls own behavior.	Usually controls own behavior.	Often does not control own behavior.

Figure 2.6. Analytic Rubric for Encouraging a Friend to Participate

Specific Behavior	Levels of Performance		
	3: Terrific	2: Okay	1: Needs Work
Asks the friend to participate.	Often the student says things like, "What do you think about ___?", "Can you draw the _____?" "Would you please make the _____?" Each question is specific to the task at hand.	Sometimes the student asks questions pertinent to the task to engage other students.	The student seldom asks questions.
Listens actively.	Always looks at the speaker and does not talk when someone else is talking.	Usually looks at the speaker and does not talk when someone else is talking.	Often does not look at the speaker. Often talks when someone else is talking.
Is courteous and polite.	Always says "please" and "thank you" and uses other polite language. Never uses impolite language.	Often says "please" and "thank you" and uses other polite language. Never uses impolite language.	Usually does not say "please" and "thank you," and usually does not use other polite language. The student may also use impolite language.
Acts friendly.	Smiles when appropriate and is usually kind.	Smiles when appropriate and is often kind.	Usually does not smile and is seldom kind. May be unkind.
Keeps hands and feet to self.	Always keeps hands and feet to self.	Usually keeps hands and feet to self.	Often is inappropriate in the use of hands and feet.

Creating Assessment Lists from Analytic Rubrics and T Charts

Strategy of Creating Assessment Lists

The assessment list is a tool to help students pay attention to their behavior, skills, and class work. It contains items that are relevant to the general skill, behavior, or work being assessed and has a reasonable number of items that students will be able to pay attention to. In the beginning, an assessment list may only contain one item because the students are ready to pay attention to only one thing. When the students are comfortable with one-item assessment lists, then the teacher adds one or two items more. Assessment lists are usually never more than four or five items long in the primary grades.

On a four-item assessment list, two or three of the items describe specific skills or behaviors that are "sure things," i.e., behaviors or skills with which the students are comfortable and perform at the "Terrific" or "Okay" level. Paying attention to these behaviors or skills is encouraging to the students and reinforces positive behavior.

One item on the assessment list is a "challenge" because most of the students are performing at the "Needs Work" level on that item. By placing a "challenge" item on the assessment list, the teacher has selected a focus for instruction and improvement in student performance. Classroom time will be devoted to discussions, demonstrations, modeling, and practice of this skill or behavior.

The "T" Chart shown in Figure 2.1 is about following classroom routines. Three items in the "T" Chart are marked "ST" and one is marked "C" by a teacher who used the "T" chart to assess the overall strengths and needs of her students before she created the assessment list in Figure 2.7.

That same teacher could have used the analytic rubric in Figure 2.4 and circled the levels of behavior of her students relevant to following classroom routines in preparation for creating the assessment list. Then that information could have been used to create the assessment list in Figure 2.7.

When students are familiar with assessment lists, involve them in reviewing the "T" charts and helping to create assessment lists with "sure things" and "challenges."

Summary of the Steps in Creating an Assessment List

- ◆ Select a general behavior or work habit to assess.
- ◆ Use a "T" Chart or an Analytic Rubric to describe the specific skills or specific observable behaviors relevant to the general behavior or work habit.

- Select one to three specific skills or observable behaviors on which the students do very well. These will be the "Sure Thing" items on the assessment list.
- Select one specific skill or observable behavior on which the students do poorly. This will be the "Challenge" item on the assessment list.
- Write the items on the assessment list, putting the Challenge item in the middle of the list.
- Write the items on the assessment list in the form of questions that the student will ask him or herself during self-assessment.
- Assure that the items are stated in student's language and are short and to the point.
- Never make more than one page of assessment list items—four or five items—for students in the early grade levels. In the beginning, the assessment list may be only one or two items long.

Formats for Assessment Lists

Figures 2.7, 2.8, and 2.9 show a format for assessment lists. Here the assessment list is on one piece of paper that can be used by individual or small groups of students. Other formats for assessment lists include:

- Large wall posters
- Sentence strip holders with one item on each strip
- Activity center posters
- Small, individual assessment lists taped to the student's desk or in his or her homework folder or journal

Figure 2.7. Performance Task Assessment List: Following Classroom Routines

1. Did I look at the teacher when I heard and saw the Stop-Look-Listen sign?

    Terrific   OK   Needs Work

2. Did I move quietly to where I should be in the classroom?

    Terrific   OK   Needs Work

3. Did I use my whisper voice when I was thinking out loud?

    Terrific   OK   Needs Work

4. Did I use my quiet sharing voice when I was in my group?

    Terrific   OK   Needs Work

Figure 2.8. Performance Task Assessment List:
Following Directions for the Task

1. Did I look at the teacher when the directions were given?

2. Was I quiet when the directions were given?

3. Did I raise my hand if I had a question?

4. Did I get the materials that I needed?

Figure 2.9. Performance Task Assessment List: Encouraging My Friend to Participate

1. Did I look at my friend and smile?

    Terrific   OK   Needs Work

2. Did I ask my friend a question about the topic?

    Terrific   OK   Needs Work

3. Did I keep quiet when my friend was talking?

    Terrific   OK   Needs Work

4. Did I say, "Thank you" to my friend?

    Terrific   OK   Needs Work

Using Assessment Lists

The act of creating the assessment list helps the teacher become more focused on what he expects of the students. The assessment list communicates and clarifies those expectations to the students.

Prior to the use of an assessment list, the teacher has verbally taught the students the behaviors or skills included on the assessment list. Although a student may not be "Terrific" or even "Okay" regarding a specific behavior or skill, the student understands what is meant by each item on the assessment list.

The students review the assessment list before they are about to engage in the behavior, skill, or work relevant to that assessment list. For example, the assessment list for classroom routines would be introduced at the beginning of the day and an assessment list for following directions would be introduced at the beginning of an activity where following directions was especially important. An assessment list for encouraging participation of a friend would be introduced before a cooperative learning activity.

As the students are engaged in the activity the teacher uses the assessment list to refocus their attention on the specific behaviors and skills to which they should attend.

Immediately at the end of the activity, the teacher and the class review the assessment list and talk about whether the performance was "Terrific," "Okay," or at the "Needs Work" level. The teacher may ask, "How did we do on paying attention to the teacher?" and regardless of the response the students give, the teacher says, "Tell me what we did that showed that we were (Terrific, Okay, or Needs Work.)" The teacher needs the students to judge their behavior or skill level and to justify that judgment with "evidence" of their actual performance.

Initially, when introducing the use of assessment lists, students may not be accurate in judging the quality of their own performance. A strategy is to focus on one or two items in which the students are very accurate. This kind of an assessment list item is called a "Sure Thing" because students will most likely do very well on it. When the students accurately assess their work on the "Sure Thing" items, a more difficult item can be introduced to the assessment list. Persistence and patience usually result in success.

In the case of classroom behaviors presented in this chapter, students usually do not get individual assessment lists. Whole group discussions are held using a large classroom assessment list poster or in a sentence-strip chart.

If a student is particularly weak in a behavior or skill, the student might receive an individualized two-item assessment list. One of the items would be on a behavior that the student has mastered and the second item would focus on a behavior in need of improvement. This two-item assessment list is used in addition to the whole-class assessment list poster or sentence-strip chart.

Using Models Of Desired Behaviors

"T" Charts, analytic rubrics, and assessment lists on their own are not sufficient to coach students to improve their performance. Students must see and hear examples, models, or benchmarks of excellent performance. Models can be in the format of a video; photographs; audio tape; or actual examples of student work such as drawings, writing, constructions, and computer-generated products. Videos of students carrying out classroom routines, following directions for an independent task, or working in a cooperative group can provide examples of expected levels of behavior. Skits can show "Terrific," "Okay," and "Needs Work" levels of performance. Actual student work samples can be used as benchmarks of quality.

Classroom discussions about what is seen and heard in these videos and skits help focus students' attention on what to do and how well to do it. Some teachers have their students use the assessment list to judge the quality of the behaviors presented in the videos or skits so that the students experience connecting the items in the assessment list to actual performance.

Setting Goals (Standards of Performance) for Student Performance Regarding Desired Behaviors

The models or benchmarks of student performance show the "Terrific," "Okay," and "Needs Work" levels of performance. Models or benchmarks should set goals for performance. A video of students doing a terrific job of following classroom routines or a student's terrific drawing of a scene from a story with written explanation help define what quality is.

Models of "Okay" or "Needs Work" levels of performance are sometimes used to help students compare and contrast between these levels and a "Terrific" performance. Care must be taken not to offend students by showing their behavior or work as "not Terrific." Sometimes, simulations or skits are videotaped to be used as the less-than-Terrific levels of performance. Sometimes the teacher "creates" the flawed samples to use as a model of "Needs Work" so as not to embarrass any student.

Teachers save samples of student work from past years, with names removed, to use as models of excellent work and models with flaws.

Mantra of Self-Reflection: What?—So What?—Now What?

The goal of using assessment is to coach the student to take responsibility for accurately assessing his or her own work and then to set and carry out goals to improve their own performance. The teacher's job is to coach the students to learn to ask and answer these questions:

- ◆ **What** was my task?
- ◆ **What** is terrific work like?
- ◆ **So what** are the strengths of my work?
- ◆ **So what** do I need to improve on?
- ◆ **Now what** am I going to do to get better?

Differentiating Instruction and Assessment

Students in our classrooms differ widely, and assessment lists, and strategies to use those lists, can be differentiated to meet some individualized needs. In some situations, the same assessment list can be used for the whole class. In other situations, two or three versions of the assessment list may be used. Regarding the general behavior of following classroom routines, students may differ regarding their areas of deficiency. One assessment list may include the challenge item of "moving quietly to the new activity" and another version of the assessment list may include the challenge item of "using my quiet sharing voice when I am in a center with a friend."

An alternative to using more than one version of an assessment list is to have these two challenge items on one list and circle one for one student and the other for the second student.

The Long-Term Goal Regarding Using Assessment Lists

The ultimate goal of using assessment lists is not to get students good at using the assessment lists we create. The goal is for students to internalize the process of thinking about quality before they begin their work, during their work, and at the conclusion of their work. We want students to use the "assessment lists in their heads." Steps along the way to this goal for students include getting good at assessment lists provided by teachers, helping to make assessment lists, making their own assessment lists, and using an internalized assessment list.

In the primary grades we begin this process, which empowers students to become motivated, independent learners who take responsibility for the quality of their behavior and work.

Glossary Of Terms

Analytic Rubric: A type of assessment tool that lists all the specific attributes or elements of a performance and provides narrative descriptions of several levels of performance for each of those attributes or elements. An analytic rubric for a complex behavior such as "Following Classroom Routines" may have six or more elements. In the context of this book, narrative descriptors define "Terrific," "Okay," and "Needs Work" performance for each of these elements.

An analytic rubric is created and used for the year or many years as a consistent framework to view student performance.

Assessment List: A type of assessment tool that lists a few of the many possible attributes or elements of the performance. An assessment list for "Following Classroom Routines" may have only three or four items because that is the maximum number of items the students are ready to pay attention to at the time the assessment list was created. Assessment lists are written by the teacher, often with input from the students. Assessment lists are developed for specific tasks and are changed often as students master some behaviors or skills and shift their attention to new learning.

Although the analytic rubric, once created, remains unchanged for a long time, the assessment lists change often based on the behaviors and skills to which the students should attend.

Model: A model is an example of the behavior (active listening) or work (drawing a picture and writing a sentence about it) being examined with the help of an assessment tool. (Synonyms for the term "model" include example, benchmark, and standard of quality.) Models usually show the high goal for the exhibition of the behavior or skill. Models for "flawed" work are sometimes used to help point out the strengths of the good work through comparing and contrasting models of excellence with the flawed examples.

Performance-Based Learning and Assessment: *Assessment* is the gathering of information about what students know and are able to do. Performance assessment focuses on the application of knowledge and skills. The strategies in this book are called "performance-based learning and assessment" because the activities used as the basis for assessment are both learning activities and opportunities to assess student performance.

Self-Assessment: Students use assessment lists and their knowledge of models (benchmarks) to identify their own strengths and needs. Teachers coach students to learn to be accurate self-assessors.

Self-Regulation: Through self-regulation, students set and carry out goals to improve their performance. Teachers coach students to set realistic goals and action plans to improve. This drives the instruction for another cycle of work that culminates with another round of self-assessment and self-regulation.

Standards of Performance: Each type of behavior, such as following classroom routines, encouraging friends to participate in group work, and following directions is manifested in a range of actual student performance. Standard of performance, i.e., standard of quality, is set to define the high goal towards which to strive. Models of student performance, including videos of actual performance, are used to define these standards of performance.

"T" Chart: A "T" Chart is a tool used by teachers to help students identify the specific outcomes of their behavior or work that then can be used to create assessment tools.

3

Teaching and Assessing Reading Comprehension Through Teacher-Led Discussions in Various Types of Reading Groups

Topics in This Chapter

♦ Strategies to create questions based on the framework for reading comprehension for use during various reading group activities.

♦ Strategies to create tools to assess and evaluate reading comprehension exhibited by students during group reading activities.

Levels of Reading Comprehension

Comprehension can be thought of as a continuum from barely understanding the simple facts of a story to a deeper understanding of the author's "message" of the book and how the story connects to the reader's own life.

This book uses a four-level framework for reading comprehension as described by the National Assessment of Education Progress (NAEP). The first level is called **Literal Understanding** and refers to the degree to which students understand the basic facts of the book. At this level the students identify the main characters, describe the setting as shown in the illustrations, and retell the story.

The second level of comprehension is called **Developing an Interpretation** and refers to the degree to which students can use thinking skills such as predicting what comes next in the story and finding evidence to show that a character exhibited an attribute such as friendship or bravery.

The third level of comprehension is called **Making Connections** and refers to the degree to which the students can use thinking skills such as comparing one story to another, and comparing an event in a story to an event in their own lives. The connections are "text-to-me," "text-to-text," and "text-to-world."

The fourth level of comprehension is called **Critical Stance**. For fiction books, Critical Stance refers to the degree to which students form an opinion and support it. This is where a student may share whether he liked or disliked the story, the characters or the illustrations and be able to explain why. For nonfiction books, Critical Stance refers to the degree to which students form an opinion on how useful and interesting the information in the book was.

Figure 3.1 shows the relationship among the four levels of comprehension. Literal Understanding is at the center of comprehension because if you do not know the facts, the higher levels of comprehension will be more difficult to achieve. The other three levels are shown in a circle beyond Literal Understanding. Developing an Interpretation, Making Connections, and Critical Stance all represent thinking that is of a higher order than Literal Understanding. Initial Understanding is the foundation on which higher-order thinking is based.

Figure 3.1. Four Levels of Reading Comprehension

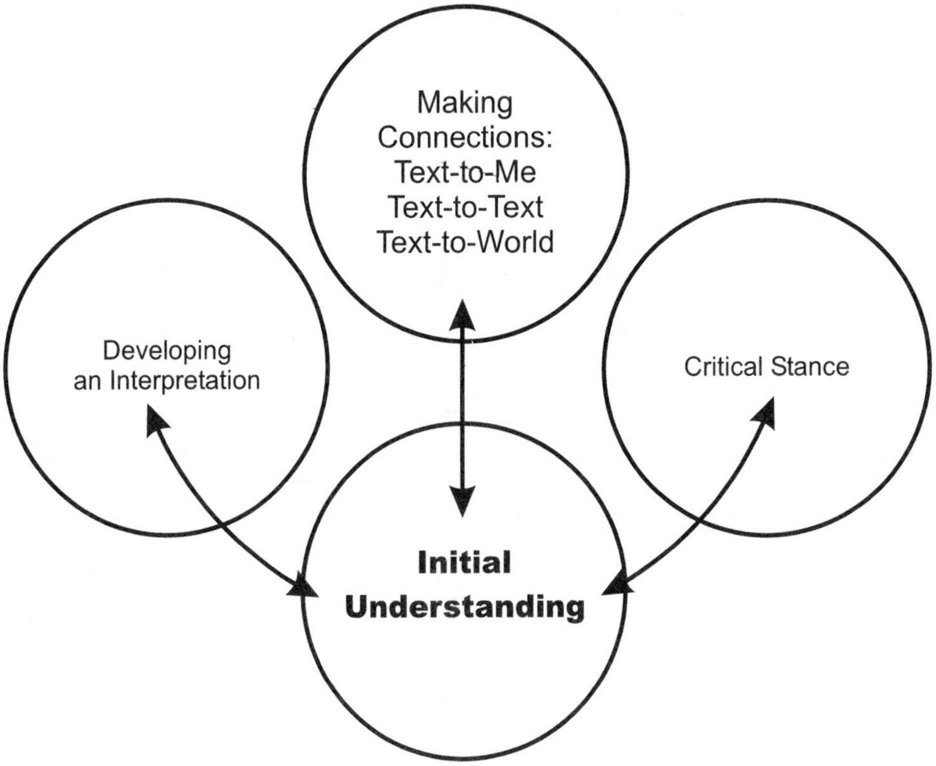

Generating Questions Based on the Levels of Understanding for Use During Group Reading Activities

A set of questions based on the four levels of reading comprehension should be developed for each book. Care should be taken to develop questions at all four levels of comprehension. Common mistakes include having too many questions at the Initial Understanding level and too few questions at the Critical Stance level.

Figure 3.2 presents a "handy" graphic to help guide in the development of questions. Who, What, Where and Story Events are the basis for Initial Understanding questions. The Problem, Solution/Ending, and What The Story Is Mostly About are the basis for Developing an Interpretation questions. The ring finger reminds us to create Making Connections questions. The little finger reminds us to ask the students to explain what they liked/disliked about the way the author and illustrator told the story. Figure 3.3 provides sample reading comprehension questions for several books.

Figure 3.2. Handy Graphic for Reading Comprehension

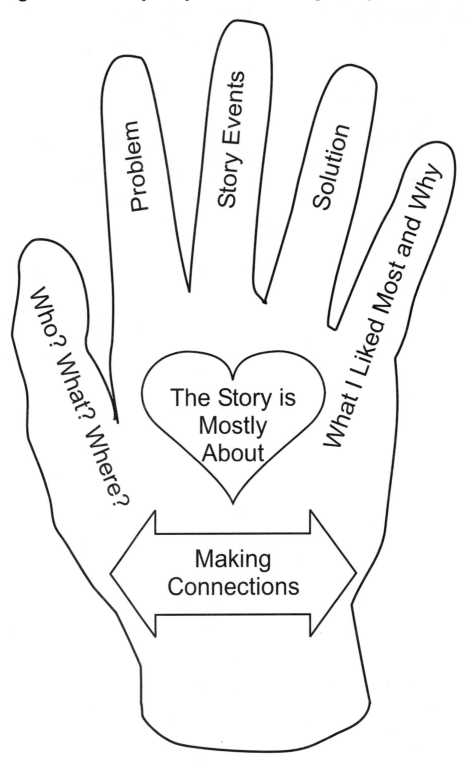

Figure 3.3. Sample Reading Comprehension Questions

Level of Comprehension	Arthur's Birthday
	by Marc Brown
Initial Understanding	• Who had a birthday in the story? • What was Arthur's favorite flavor for his birthday cake? • Where did Arthur and Francine write birthday invitations?
Developing an Interpretation	• What was the problem? • Did the boys and girls like each other? • How did the story end so that the problem was solved?
Making Connections	• Have you ever had a problem with your birthday party? • How did you solve the problem?
Critical Stance	• Which picture in the story does the best job of showing that Arthur and Muffy were friends?

Level of Comprehension	Arthur Lost And Found
	by Marc Brown
Initial Understanding	• Who went on the bus with Arthur? • What were the boys doing on the bus? • Where did the boys go on the bus?
Developing an Interpretation	• How did Arthur feel about taking a bus ride? • How did Arthur's mother feel when she found out that Arthur was not at the pool?
Making Connections	• Have you ever been lost and how were you found? • What kind things have bus drivers done for you?
Critical Stance	• What part of the story was most interesting to you? • Why?

Level of Comprehension	*Arthur's Tooth*
	by Marc Brown
Initial Understanding	• Who had a loose tooth? • What did Arthur want to loose? • Where did Arthur loose his tooth?
Developing an Interpretation	• How did Arthur feel about going to the dentist? • Who was most helpful to Arthur?
Making Connections	• Do you want to loose your baby teeth? • Why? • How did you loose a tooth?
Critical Stance	• Do you think that the author, Marc Brown, showed a real way a person could loose a tooth?

Level of Comprehension	*Franklin and the Tooth Fairy*
	by Paulette Bourgeous and Benda Clark
Initial Understanding	• Who was Franklin's best friend? • What did Bear have that Franklin did not have? • Where did the Tooth Fairy leave presents?
Developing an Interpretation	• What problem was Franklin having? • How did Franklin's parents help him solve his problem?
Making Connections	• What problem about teeth did both Franklin and Arthur have? • How were the tooth fairy presents in the story like the presents you get for your teeth?
Critical Stance	• Did you like the way the authors showed the tooth fairy? • Why or why not.

Level of Comprehension	Franklin's New Friend
	by Paulette Bourgeous and Benda Clark
Initial Understanding	• Who was Franklin's new friend? • What did the Moose do to help the other children? • Where did Franklin and Moose play?
Developing an Interpretation	• Why was Franklin afraid? • Did Moose feel good when he first came to school?
Making Connections	• Have you ever been a little scared about making new friends? • What have you done to make a new friend feel good?
Critical Stance	• Do you think that this story is like the way things really are when new students come to school? • Why or why not?

Level of Comprehension	Franklin Wants A Pet
	by Paulette Bourgeous and Benda Clark
Initial Understanding	• What did Franklin want? • Who told Franklin "We'll think about it?" • What were some of the pets that Franklin did not want? • What pet did Franklin choose?
Developing an Interpretation	• Why were Franklin's parents concerned about a pet? • Was Franklin careful about selecting a pet? • How do you know?
Making Connections	• What kind of a pet would you want? Why? • What kind of pet do you have? • What are some reasons that your parents might not want to have pets in the house?
Critical Stance	• Do you think that the author showed how parents usually feel about getting pets for their children? • Why or why not?

Using "T" Charts to Generate Ideas to Assess Student Comprehension During Reading Group Activities

Chapter 2 introduced the use of "T" charts to identify the specific "looks like" and "sounds like" behavior that would be evidence that a certain overall behavior was being carried out well. Chapter 2 dealt with the overall behaviors of classroom skills, individual task skills, and cooperative learning group skills. This chapter uses a "T" chart to identify the specific behaviors relevant to demonstrating reading comprehension during reading group activities.

"T" charts like the one in Figure 3.4 are created by teachers visualizing what it is like to sit in front of a reading group and see and hear students showing a high level of reading comprehension. A comparison between Figures 3.2 and 3.4 shows that all the "handy" reminders are covered in the "T" chart.

Figure 3.4. Behaviors Important to Demonstrating Reading Comprehension in Shared Reading Groups

When I comprehend what I read

it looks like:	*it sounds like:*
The students are looking at the book.	The students are quiet except when participating directly in the shared reading.
The student is pointing at the correct word or picture when asked to come up to participate.	The students, as a group, are saying the words correctly when the words are pointed to.
When asked, the student points to the words, one at a time, as the story or poem is read.	A student says the words correctly when he or she comes up to the big book to participate.
The students' mouths are not moving except when they are participating in the shared reading activities.	When called on, the student retells a piece of the story or answers the who, when, or where questions.
The students are keeping their hands and feet to themselves.	The student makes a prediction as to what will happen next. The student tells what clues are used to make a prediction.
The students are looking at the student who is speaking.	The student correctly answers the questions, "What is the story mostly about?" "What is the problem in this story?" or "How did the story end?" or "How does this story remind you of another story we read?" or "How does this story remind you of something that happened to you?"
	The student explains what was best or most interesting about the story.

Making Assessment Lists for Reading Comprehension from "T" Charts

The purpose of an assessment list is to get the students to pay attention to the quality of their work. The assessment list items must be shared and discussed with the students just before they engage in the activity through which their performance will be assessed. If an assessment list is to be used during a shared reading group, then the items on that list must be discussed during the first part of that group activity.

The strategy proposed in this chapter is to use sentence strip holders and print one assessment list item on each strip. One strip presents the three faces and the words "Terrific," "Okay," and "Needs Work." One strip with an assessment item is followed by a strip with the faces and words.

In the beginning, possibly only one assessment item is used and as students get more experienced with the assessment items in the sentence strip holders several assessment items can be used for a shared reading activity.

Figures 3.5, 3.6, and 3.7 show sentence strip holders for a whole class reading activity. Figure 3.5 represents a sentence strip holder with one assessment item and its companion strip of faces and words. Figure 3.6 shows two assessment items sharing a face and word strip, and Figure 3.7 shows the holder with four assessment list items and two strips of faces.

Figure 3.5. Sentence Strip Holder with One Assessment Item

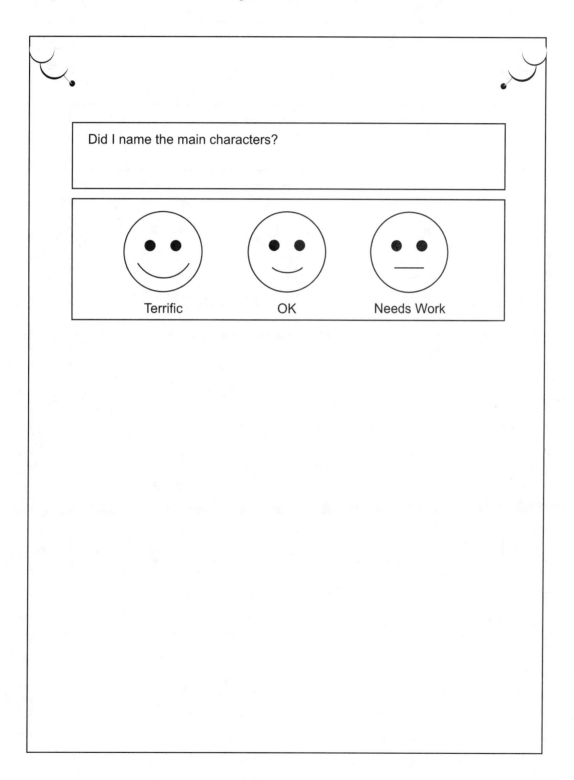

Did I name the main characters?

Terrific   OK   Needs Work

Figure 3.6. Sentence Strip Holder with Two Assessment Items

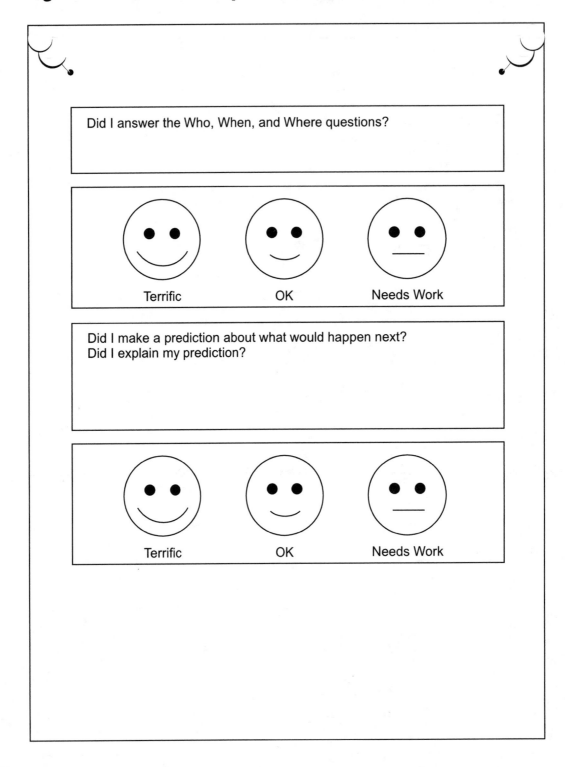

Figure 3.7. Sentence Strip Holder with Four Assessment Items

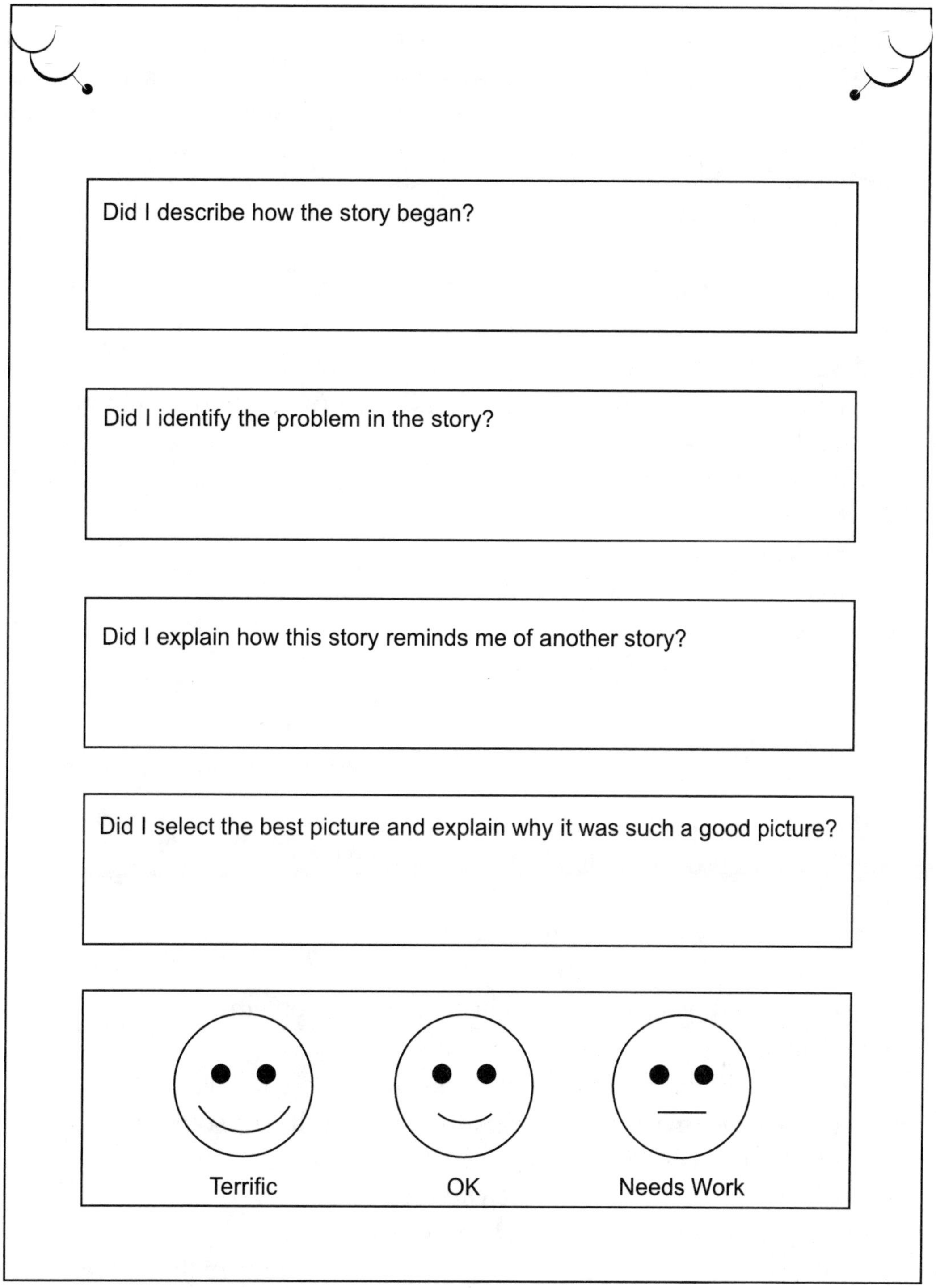

Did I describe how the story began?

Did I identify the problem in the story?

Did I explain how this story reminds me of another story?

Did I select the best picture and explain why it was such a good picture?

Terrific   OK   Needs Work

Sample Sentence Strip Assessment Items Regarding Comprehension of the Information in a Story

Students should be engaged in all four levels of reading comprehension during the study of a book. Following are samples of assessment list items organized according to their level of understanding. Consider this a menu from which to draw to construct a sentence strip chart to help students pay better attention before, during, and after reading group is done.

Initial Understanding (literal understanding of the text and illustrations)

- who is the main character?
- who re the other characters?
- where is the story happening?
- describe the setting?
- when did (night, day, winter, summer, morning, afternoon, night, etc.) the story took place?
- who, when, where?
- who did what?
- who said what?
- answer the Who, When, and Where questions?
- answer the question, "What comes next in the story?"
- describe the events in the story?
- describe how the story began?
- describe where the story began?
- describe how the story ended?
- describe where the story ended?

Developing an Interpretation (going beyond the facts in the story)

- explain what the story is mostly about?
- predict what would happened next?
- identify the problem in the story?
- explain the illustration that shows what the problem was?
- explain if this story is fantasy or real?
- explain what this author did to make this story a fantasy?
- explain if the (main character) is (brave, friendly, or some other attribute of human nature)?
- explain how _____ felt about _____?
- explain who was (most helpful, least helpful, etc.)?
- explain the cues I used to _____ (any of the above)?

Making Connections (the text-to-me, text-to-text, text-to-the-world)
Did I:

- ♦ explain how this story reminded me of another story?
- ♦ explain how this story reminded me of something that happened to me?
- ♦ explain how I am the same as (or different from) _____ (a character in the story)?
- ♦ explain how I had a similar problem?
- ♦ explain how I solved the problem like _____ (a character)?
- ♦ explain how _____ (a character in this book) is like _____ (a character in a different book)?
- ♦ explain how what happened in _____ (this story) is like or different from _____ (a different story)?
- ♦ explain how the pattern of this book (format, story line, or rhythmic pattern) is like the pattern of _____ (another book.)
- ♦ explain how the setting of _____ (this book) is like or different than the setting of _____ (another book)?
- ♦ explain the cues in the story that I used to _____ (any of the above)?

Critical Stance (being a critic of the author and illustrator)
Did I:

- ♦ explain what I liked most about the story?
- ♦ explain what character I liked (or didn't like) the most?
- ♦ judge the best illustration and explain why it is so good?
- ♦ explain what the author did to make this story so interesting?
- ♦ explain what the illustrator did to make this story so interesting?
- ♦ explain why I think the author did a good job of telling the story?
- ♦ explain why I think the illustrator did a good job telling the story?
- ♦ rate the books (during an author study) written by _____ and explain why I liked the book _____ the best?

Sample Sentence Strip Assessment Items Regarding Concepts of Print, Cueing Systems and Behavior

In addition to assessing comprehension of the story, the students' understanding of the concepts of print, the use of cueing systems, and behavior during group reading activities can be assessed using sentence strip assessment strategies. Following are some sample sentence strip assessment items for these aspects of student performance.

Concepts of Print
Did I:

- point to the words that are being read?
- return sweep?

Cueing Systems
Did I:

- look at the picture?
- look for chunks I know?
- reread?
- get my lips ready to say the word?
- think, "Does it look right?", "Does it sound right?" and "Does it make sense?"

Behavior
Did I:

- keep my hands and feet to myself?
- sit quietly and pay attention to the book?
- look at the pictures?
- use cueing systems to help me figure out a word?
- say what strategy I used to figure out a word?
- read in my whisper voice when I should?
- use my large group-sharing voice when it was my turn to read?

Strategies for Using Assessment Items in Sentence Strips During Group Reading Activities

The following are suggestions for using assessment items in sentence strip holders before, during, and after shared reading activities.

- Meet with the students at the group reading area, e.g., the rug or the easel.
- Put the assessment list items into the sentence strip holder one at a time. Sometimes only one assessment list item is used for a shared reading activity. Never more than four assessment list items are used for any one shared reading activity.
- Have a class discussion as to the meaning of the smiley faces for "Terrific," "Okay," and "Needs Work."
- Have a class discussion on the meaning of each item before another item is put into the sentence strip holder. The discussion about an assessment list item may include modeling by you and ideas from the students.
- Engage in shared reading.

- Every so often, stop and direct the students' attention to a particular assessment list item. Additional modeling and/or class discussion may ensue. You may ask the students to assess how they are doing "so far" regarding the assessment list item.

- When the shared reading is completed return to the sentence strip holder. The group as a whole assess their overall performance on each item.

- Ask the students to select one item from the sentence strip holder on which to improve. That item is marked with a clothes pin or some other visible marker. This marked item is then the center of discussion.

- Elicit ideas from the students as to how they can improve their performance regarding that one assessment list item.

- When students are accurate in their self-assessment and have good ideas to improve their performance, recognize and encourage that effort.

- When the students are inaccurate in their self-assessment, describe what you saw and heard (focusing the students' attention on the relevant behaviors) and then ask for a reassessment. Then verbalize your opinion of the quality of performance relevant to that assessment list item and model the correct performance.

- The item marked with the clothes pin becomes the first item discussed during the next shared reading activity.

- Practice, practice, practice.

- Patience

Glossary of Terms

Assessment is the act of collecting data about student performance. The data may be in the form of a rating of Terrific, Okay, or Needs Work concerning a student's behavior in group work, or that student's ability to retell a story, or the student's use of details in the drawing of the main character in the book.

Evaluation is the interpretation a teacher places on the data acquired through assessment. One student may be assessed as Okay regarding his or her work and the teacher may evaluate that level of performance as "good news" because it represents an improvement in the student's performance. A second student may be assessed as Okay on the same work and the teacher may evaluate that level of performance as "not so good news" because it represents a regression in performance for that student.

Guided Reading according to Fountas and Pinnell is, "...a context in which a teacher supports each reader's development of effective strategies for processing novel texts at increasingly challenging levels of difficulty." Carol Ann

Burgner and Christine Murphy explain the process of conducting guided reading groups this way: "The teacher brings together a small group of children who are similar in reading development. Based on observation, the teacher forms groups, and for a small period of the language arts block, children are reading with a group of their peers who have similar reading behaviors and are reading at just about the same level. Note that the grouping for guided reading is a dynamic process. As children grow, there will be variations in their rate of progress and in the nature of the understandings they develop, so the groupings need to change. Children are grouped and regrouped through the use of observation as an integral part of the process."

Levels of Reading Comprehension. The basic level of reading comprehension is Literal Understanding, where students do such things as retell a story, identify main characters, and describe the setting. Higher-order thinking includes making predictions, inferences, and comparisons; connecting information in the reading to personal experience; and judging or evaluating the author and illustrator's work. The levels of comprehension are introduced in this chapter and then defined and used in greater depth in the following chapters. This framework for Reading Comprehension comes from the National Assessment of Education Progress (NAEP.)

Initial Understanding
This level looks at the degree to which the reader has literal understanding of what was read. The student reader may be asked to demonstrate understanding by describing, listing, and/or sequencing information from the text.

Developing an Interpretation
This level looks at the degree to which the reader can extend the meaning beyond literal understanding. Here the student may be asked to demonstrate understanding through inferring, predicting, finding causes and effects, and making generalizations. Developing an Interpretation is based on one source of information, such as information in one story.

Making Connections
This level also looks at the degree to which the reader can extend the meaning beyond literal understanding. Here the student reader may be asked to demonstrate understanding through comparing, contrasting, inferring, predicting, finding causes and effects, and making generalizations. Making Connections is based on two or more sources of information. Here students would work with two or more books, a text and personal experience, or a text and a multimedia source. Often for Making Connections, the reader is asked to connect something in the book to something in his or her own life.

Critical Stance

This level looks at the degree to which students are able to evaluate the quality of the author. For fiction this usually means asking the student reader to judge how well the author and/or illustrator used literary devices and illustrations to tell an effective story. For nonfiction this usually means asking the student reader to judge the accuracy and objectivity of factual information. Here the student reader may be asked to demonstrate understanding through judging, evaluating, assessing, rating, and ranking.

Read-Alouds are when the teacher reads a story to the students. Most Read-Alouds are conducted with the whole class. The book may be in a "big book" format or regular size. The teacher may occasionally model some reading comprehension strategies and asks students some questions about the story. Library/media teachers also use this strategy extensively.

Shared Reading is when the teacher uses a "big book" to engage the students in a whole group activity. (Sometimes, shared reading can be used when the teacher uses a small text and each student has his or her own copy.) The setting for shared reading looks like the setting for read-alouds. The students may do some of the reading. The teacher models reading comprehension strategies and engages the students in questions at the various levels of reading comprehension. For, example the teacher may ask for a retelling of a part of the story, ask for predictions of what will come next, ask for a connection between the story and a student's own experiences, and ask for what the students liked about the illustrations.

References

Bourgeois, P., & Clark, B. (1995). *Franklin wants a pet*. New York: Scholastic.

Bourgeois, P., & Clark, B. (1996). *Franklin and the Tooth Fairy*. New York: Scholastic.

Bourgeois, P., & Clark, B. (1997). *Franklin's new friend*. New York: Scholastic.

Brown, M. (1985). *Arthur's tooth*. New York: Scholastic.

Brown, M. (1989). *Arthur's birthday*. New York: Scholastic.

Brown, M. (1998). *Arthur lost and found*. New York: Scholastic.

4

Teaching and Assessing Reading Comprehension of Fiction Through Drawing

Topics in This Chapter

- Strategies for using a framework for reading comprehension that focuses on thinking-skill verbs to make performance tasks asking students to draw and present orally.
- Strategies to make analytic rubrics and assessment lists for judging the quality of drawings and oral presentations.
- Strategies to use performance tasks and assessment tools in the context of language arts lessons.

Careful Observation Is a Foundation for Understanding

Careful reading for literal understanding and careful observation of illustrations are the foundation for deeper levels of understanding. Inferences, comparisons, and evaluations can only be done if the basic information in the text is understood. In this chapter, performance tasks at all four levels of comprehension ask the student to make drawings to show their understanding of the information in the books. Then students are asked to describe their drawings to their classmates. Assessment lists are used for both the drawings and the oral presentations.

Principles and Elements of Design

An artist has a concept in mind for his or her drawing. The concept might be to convey something like "the beauty of a tree," "a scary feeling," "a proud moment," or the "love of a family member." Figure 4.1 presents a chart of the principles and elements of design. The student artist makes decisions about how to use a principle such as "Emphasis" to help present the concept. For example, the student artist may wish to emphasize a brave action taken by a character. Then the artist uses an element such as color to carry out the principle. For example strong, bold, bright colors may help provide the emphasis to the brave action that is to be highlighted.

The chart in Figure 4.1 can be a source of ideas for assessment list items. It is presented in a matrix form so that decisions can be made as to which elements will be used to accomplish which principles. For example, a teacher has used the chart in Figure 4.1 to select the principle of "Emphasis" and the elements of "Color" and "Value" to accomplish that principle. The performance task and its assessment list will incorporate the use of color and value to accomplish emphasis. Figures 4.11 and 4.13 show the performance task titled, "Brave Max" and its two assessment lists that ask the student to use strong bright colors to emphasize Max's brave action and then to describe the drawing orally to the class. In this chapter, each task has an assessment list for the drawing and a separate assessment list for the oral presentation. Collaborate with an art teacher when you use principles and elements of design as part of the instruction and assessment of student drawing.

Principles of Design

- ◆ **Pattern**: This refers to the combination of lines, colors, shapes used to show real or imaginary things, and is also achieved by repeating a line, color, or shape etc.
- ◆ **Movement**: This refers to the arrangement of parts in a drawing to create a slow-to-fast flow of your eyes through the work.
- ◆ **Balance**: This refers to the equalization of elements. Types of balance include symmetrical (equal on both sides), asymmetrical (balanced but unequal in number), and radial or central (spokes on a wheel or rays on a sun.)
- ◆ **Unity**: This refers to the sense of oneness or wholeness in a work or art.
- ◆ **Contrast**: This refers to different values, colors, textures, and other elements in an art work used to achieve emphasis and interest.
- ◆ **Rhythm**: This indicates the type of movement in an artwork or design often by repeating shapes.
- ◆ **Emphasis**: This concerns defining a central point or points to which the eyes are drawn.

Elements of Design

Elements of design are used to accomplish the Principles:

♦ **Texture**: This refers to the surface quality of an artwork—the way it "feels" such as rough, smooth, bumpy, fuzzy, hard, or soft.

♦ **Shape**: This is defined by a two-dimensional and enclosed space. Geometric shapes include circles, squares, triangles, and many more. Organic shapes are freeform or shapes from nature such as maple leaf-shape or pine tree-shape.

♦ **Form**: This refers to a three-dimensional, enclosed volume such as a cylinder, cube, or sphere.

♦ **Line**: This may be two-dimensional such as a pencil line on paper or three-dimensional line using a rope or wire.

♦ **Value**: This refers to the lightness or darkness of a color.

♦ **Space**: This refers to either the positive area of an object or the negative space where the object isn't.

♦ **Color**: This refers to the hue (red, yellow, violet). The primary colors are blue, yellow, and red. The secondary colors are green, orange and violet.

Figure 4.1. Principles and Elements of Design: Used To Help The Artist Convey His or Her Concepts and Ideas

Principles of Design	Elements of Design Used to Accomplish Principles						
	Texture	Shape	Form	Line	Color	Value	Space
Pattern							
Movement							
Balance							
Unity							
Contrast							
Rhythm							
Emphasis					X	X	

Analytic Rubrics for Drawing and Oral Presentation

Figures 4.2 and 4.3 present analytic rubrics that help teachers consider three levels of performance for the elements of drawing and speaking.

Figure 4.2. Analytic Rubric for Drawings

Specific Behavior	Levels of Performance		
	3: Terrific	2: Okay	1: Needs Work
On the topic	The drawing is clearly on the topic of the assignment.	The drawing is on the topic but may have "strayed" off the topic a little.	The drawing is off the topic.
Shows details	Just the right amount of details are used to communicate.	Either too many or not enough details are used.	There are no details or so many details are used that they obscure the main point of the drawing.
Uses colors	The student has used colors appropriately according to the assignment.	The student has mostly used colors according to the task.	The student has used colors inappropriately according to the task.
Uses proportion	The proportions are correct.	The proportions are mostly correct.	The proportions are mostly incorrect.
Shows foreround/ middleground/ background	The drawing clearly uses foreground, middleground, and background.	The student uses two of these levels, such as foreground and background only.	The student drawing is in one level; no three-dimensional effect at all.
Uses labels and words	Labels are clear and correct if needed.	Labels are mostly clear and correct.	Labels are lacking or unclear and/or incorrect.
Uses the paper	Uses the entire paper well	Uses most of the paper well	Does not use the paper well
Overall impact and creativity	Wow!!! It really gets my attention.	It gets my attention.	It is not very attention-grabbing.
Is neat	Very neat	Neat	Not neat

Figure 4.3. Analytic Rubric for Oral Descriptions of Drawings

Specific Behavior	Levels of Performance		
	3: Terrific	2: Okay	1: Needs Work
On the topic.	The presentation is entirely on the topic of the drawing. The student very clearly answers the question about the drawing.	Most of the presentation is about the drawing. The student answers the question about the drawing.	The student strays off-topic often.
Presents the drawing.	The student shows the drawing for all to see clearly.	The drawing is shown so that most of the students can see it.	The drawing is not presented well—not many students can see it.
Describes/ explains the details of the drawing.	The student includes many details in the description of the drawing.	The student includes some details in the description.	The student uses few details.
Uses descriptive language.	The student uses many descriptive words to describe the drawing.	The student uses some descriptive language.	The student uses little or no descriptive language.
Uses a loud, group-sharing voice.	The student uses a loud, group sharing voice throughout the presentation so all can hear.	The student uses a loud, group sharing voice most of the time and can be heard by most.	The student's voice is too quiet and cannot be heard.

Framing Ideas for Performance Tasks Using the Thinking-Skill Verbs.

A first step in creating performance tasks for a book is to brainstorm ideas. At least one idea for each of the levels of reading comprehension should be developed. Figure 4.4 presents a matrix of ideas for performance tasks.

Figure 4.4. Ideas for Performance Tasks

Level of Reading Comprehension	Books	
	David's Drawings	Where The Wild Things Are
Initial Understanding (The comprehension skill used for these tasks is **describe**.)	Draw a picture of David. Draw a picture of one of David's friends.	Draw a picture that shows Max getting into mischief at his home. Draw a picture of one of the "Wild Things."
Developing an Interpretation (The comprehension skill used for these tasks is **infer**.)	Draw a picture that shows that David is a friendly person.	Draw a picture that shows that Max was a brave person.
Making Connections (The comprehension skill used for these tasks is **compare**.)	Draw a picture of something you did that was like what David did.	Draw a picture that shows how you would be brave with a monster or "Wild Thing" from your own imagination.
Critical Stance (The comprehension skill used for these tasks is **judge**.)	Did Cathryn Falwell, the author, have a good ending to the story? Draw the part of the ending that you thought was good.	Did Maurice Sendak, the author, have a good beginning to the story? Draw the part of the beginning that you thought was good.

Creating Performance Tasks

Once ideas are generated for tasks, one or more of them can be turned into performance tasks with assessment lists. It is important that students be engaged in all four levels of reading comprehension: *Initial Understanding, Developing an Interpretation, Making Connections,* and *Critical Stance*. Teachers can frame many short discussion questions around the four levels of comprehension and create one or two performance tasks for a particular book. Over the course of using several books, performance tasks will address all four levels of comprehension (see Figure 4.5).

The following two tasks for *David's Drawings* address the levels of *Initial Understanding* and *Critical Stance*. The two tasks for *Where The Wild Things Are* address the levels of *Developing an Interpretation* and *Making Connections*. The one task for *Brave Irene* addresses the level of *Developing an Interpretation*.

The collection of books that addresses the theme of bravery provides materials for tasks about the bravery of boys, girls, Native Americans, and other ethnic groups women, men, and animals.

Figure 4.5. Performance Tasks for Four Levels of Comprehension

Book	*Performance Task Title*	*Comprehension Level*	*Notes To The Teacher*
David's Drawings	*David and a Friend*	IU	The drawing is of David and one of his fiends.
	A Good Ending	CS	Allow the students to select any part of the ending to show why they thought the ending was good.
Where the Wild Things Are and Brave Irene	*Brave Max* and *Brave Irene*	DI	Simply ask the students to find a part of the story that they think shows that Max was brave and draw a picture of it. Do not rephrase the task to be, "Show how Max was brave with the Wild Things." Repeat for *Brave Irene*.
	Brave Me	MC	Let the students create their own pictures that show how they imagine they would be brave in their own lives.

IU = Initial Understanding, DI = Developing An Interpretation, MC = Making Connections, CS = Critical Stance

Making Assessment Lists for the Performance Tasks

The following are some guidelines for making assessment lists for specific performance tasks:

- **Remember the Purpose of Assessment Lists:** The purpose of an assessment list is to get the students to pay attention to as much as they will pay attention to. The number of items and the wording of each item must be appropriate to this purpose.

- **Number of Items in Assessment Lists.** In the beginning, an assessment list may be only one item because that is all the students will pay attention to. Later, the students will pay attention to longer assessment lists.

- **Items Related To Task Content:** Each assessment list must have at least one item that is directly related to the content of the performance task. Item number one in the assessment list in Figure 4.7 asks the student, "Did I make a drawing of David and one of his friends?" Item number one in the assessment list in Figure 4.12 asks, "Did my picture show Max being brave?" Both of these items are about the content of the task.

- **Items Related to Task Process Skills:** Assessment lists of more than one item would also include items relevant to the process skills important to the task. Items number two and three in the assessment list in Figure 4.7 ask about the degree to which the drawing is detailed and the degree to which the student has used foreground, middleground, and background. Item number four in that same assessment list is about a work habit and asks, "Is my work neat?" All of these items are about processes important to the work.

- **Use the Analytic Rubric to Generate Items:** The analytic rubric in Figure 4.2 examines the levels of quality for the elements of a drawing. Item number two in the assessment list shown in Figure 4.7 asks, "Did I use details in my drawing?" and is derived from the second specific behavior in the analytic rubric.

- **Use the Principles and Elements of Design to Generate Items:** Item three in the assessment list in Figure 4.10 asks, "Did I use strong, bold, bright colors to help show the most interesting part of the picture?," and is derived from the chart on Elements and Principles of Design in Figure 4.1. Collaboration between regular classroom teachers and art teachers in the use of Principles and Elements of Design will support the improvement of student performance.

- **"Sure Thing" Items:** Some items must be about what the students will find easy to do because of their knowledge and skills. All the assessment lists for drawings in this chapter start with the same two "sure thing" items which ask, "Did I draw a picture of _____?" and " Did I show many details?" The teacher included these items on the assessment lists to reinforce those behaviors and encourage the students.

♦ **"Challenge" Items:** One item (in assessment lists longer than one item) on the assessment list should be a challenge for the students, i.e., something that students will find difficult to do. Item number three in the assessment list in Figure 4.12 asks, "Did I use strong, bold, bright colors to show how I was brave?" The students will need considerable instruction about what this item means before the task and assessment list are used. Unless students get prior instruction regarding challenge items, they will be unable to judge their own work in the way the challenge item calls for.

♦ **The Specificity of Items:** Challenge items must be stated in very detailed and specific terms. The following sequence of assessment list items, addressing the use of color to provide emphasis in a drawing, goes from a very specific to a general statement.

- Did I use strong, bold, bright colors to show how I was brave?
- Did I use color to show how I was brave?
- Did I use color well?

The first item in the sequence would be used for students just learning about how to use color to provide emphasis. The second item in the sequence would be used only after the students had a very good understanding that using color for emphasis meant using strong, bold, bright color. The third item in the list would be used only after students had a very good understanding that the use of color was important when creating emphasis in a drawing.

Students may need to use the most specific version of this item many times before they are ready for a more general version.

♦ **Put Items in Question Format:** The act of self-assessment is like asking questions to yourself about your work. Therefore, the assessment list items are put into question format to model that "internal conversation."

♦ **Simple Versus Complex Items**: A simple item in an assessment list might be, "Did I use details?," whereas a more complex item might involve two or more elements such as, "Did I use details and geometric shapes in my drawing?" Simple items are best for young students.

♦ **Involve Students in Helping to Create Assessment Lists**: The point of assessment lists is to coach students to take responsibility for assessing their own work and improving their performance. When possible, the students should be involved in conversations to create assessment lists.

After the students are experienced in using several assessment lists, for example, making drawings of some aspect of a story, the teacher might work with the whole group to create an assessment list for the drawing required in the next performance task.

Assessment Lists for Drawings and for Oral Descriptions of Drawings

Each task in this chapter includes an assessment list for a student's drawing. The first task, David and A Friend, has an assessment list for the student's oral description of the drawing. Subsequent performance tasks do not include an assessment list for oral presentations. Assessment lists can be used—or a sentence strip chart can be made to be used—for all oral presentations.

How Students Use Assessment Lists

The teacher explains the assessment list to the students at the beginning of the task. Assessment lists are often introduced as whole-group activities using a list that is poster-size. When the teacher feels that the students are comfortable with how assessment lists work, the students receive their own assessment list to complete. The students refer to the assessment list as they work and do a final self-assessment when their work is completed. They often circle or color in the face that represents the level of their work—Terrific, Okay, or Needs Work.

Then the teacher assesses the child's work on the same assessment list. The teacher also writes brief comments such as "I agree.", "Look at the picture of _____ (the character.)", or "I like the way you showed details." The assessment list helps both the student and the teacher focus on specific components of the work. These assessment lists are then used during conferences with the student.

Figure 4.6a. Performance Task:
David and a Friend
see the assessment lists on pages 62 and 63

Background
David is a creative, artistic student. David has many friends. Notice how each student looks in the classroom. Notice the expressions on their faces.

Task
Your task is to draw a picture of David and one of his friends together.

Audience
You will give your drawings to the librarian.

Purpose
The librarian wants to display your pictures in the library so that other students will want to read the story about David.

Procedure
1. Listen to the story as your teacher reads it.
2. Study the pictures of David and his friends.
3. Select one of David's friends to draw.
4. Draw a picture of David and one of his friends.

Figure 4.7a Performance Task:
A Good Ending
see the assessment list on page 64

Background
Good stories have strong beginnings, interesting plots, and good endings.

Task
Your task is to draw a picture that shows what you liked about the ending.

Audience
You will send your drawing to Cathryn Falwell.

Purpose
Your job is to show Cathryn Falwell what you liked about the ending.

Procedure
1. Listen to the story as your teacher reads it. Listen to how the story ends.
2. Study the pictures of the ending of the story.
3. Draw a picture that shows how the ending is good.

Figure 4.6b. Performance Task Assessment List: David and a Friend (Drawing)

1. Did I make a drawing of David and one of his friends?

2. Did I use details in my drawings?

3. Did I show foreground, middleground, and background?

4. Is my work neat?

Figure 4.6c Performance Task Assessment List:
David and a Friend (Oral Presentation of the Drawing)

1. Did I hold my drawing so that everyone could see it?

Terrific   OK   Needs Work

2. Did I use my loud sharing voice so that everyone could hear?

Terrific   OK   Needs Work

3. Did I use at least two descriptive words to describe my drawing?

Terrific   OK   Needs Work

4. Did I stay on the topic while I shared?

Terrific   OK   Needs Work

Figure 4.7b. Performance Task Assessment List:
A Good Ending (The Drawing)

1. Did I draw a picture of what I liked about the ending?

Terrific   OK   Needs Work

2. Did I show details?

Terrific   OK   Needs Work

3. Did I use strong, bold, bright colors to help show the most interesting part of the picture?

Terrific   OK   Needs Work

4. Did I do neat work?

Terrific   OK   Needs Work

Figure 4.8a. Performance Task:
Brave Max
see the assessment list on page 66

Background
Max was a brave person. He did not seem to be afraid of the Wild Things. What did Max do to show that he was brave?

Task
Your task is to draw a picture to show why you think Max is brave.

Audience
You will give your drawings to the school principal.

Purpose
Use your drawing to show the principal that you can find evidence from the story that shows Max being brave.

Procedure
1. Listen to the story as your teacher reads it.
2. Study the pictures of what Max did in the story.
3. Select one thing Max did that shows that he was brave.
4. Draw a picture of Max that shows him being brave.

Figure 4.9a. Performance Task:
Brave Irene
see the assessment list on page 67

Background
Irene was a brave person. She did not seem to be afraid of anything. What did Irene do to show that she was brave?

Task
Your task is to draw a picture that shows two things that Irene did that were brave.

Audience
You will give your drawings to the school counselor.

Purpose
Your school counselor will use your drawings to talk to other children about being brave.

Procedure
1. Listen to the story as your teacher reads it.
2. Study the pictures of what Irene did in the story.
3. Select two things that Irene did that show that she was brave.
4. Draw two pictures of Irene that show her doing a brave thing.

Figure 4.8b. Performance Task Assessment List:
Brave Max (Drawing)

1. Does my picture show Max being brave?

Terrific   OK   Needs Work

2. Did I use many details in my drawing?

Terrific   OK   Needs Work

3. Did I use strong, bold, bright colors in my drawing to show how Max was brave?

Terrific   OK   Needs Work

4. Is my work neat?

Terrific   OK   Needs Work

Figure 4.9b. Performance Task Assessment List: Brave Irene (Drawing)

1. Did each of my pictures show Irene being brave?

Terrific   OK   Needs Work

2. Did I show many details in my drawings?

Terrific   OK   Needs Work

3. Did I use strong, bold, bright colors in my drawing to show how Irene was brave?

Terrific   OK   Needs Work

4. Is my work neat?

Terrific   OK   Needs Work

Figure 4.10a. Performance Task:
Brave Me
see the assessment list on page 69

Background
Max and Irene were brave children. Are you a brave child? Do you ever imagine monsters or Wild Things or get worried about a big storm? What would you do to show that you are brave?

Task
Draw a picture that shows you being brave.

Audience
You will give your drawing to someone in your home.

Purpose
The purpose of your drawing is to show the person at home how brave you are.

Procedure
1. Listen to the stories as your teacher reads them.
2. Study the pictures that show how Max and Irene were brave.
3. Imagine how you are brave.
4. Draw a picture that shows you being brave.

Figure 4.10b. Performance Task Assessment List: Brave Me (Drawing)

1. Did I draw a picture that shows me being brave?

Terrific   OK   Needs Work

2. Did I use many details in my picture to show I was brave?

Terrific   OK   Needs Work

3. Did I use bright colors to help show how I was brave?

Terrific   OK   Needs Work

4. Is my drawing neat?

Terrific   OK   Needs Work

Using The Performance Tasks and Assessment Lists

Note: The steps of "Introducing a Book to the Whole Class Group" through and including "Using the Assessment List for the Drawing" are done on the same day. The oral presentation is done on the next day.

Before The Book Is Read

- Before the book is used, the teacher looks ahead to see what performance task and assessment list will be used.
- Based on what is emphasized in the performance task and assessment list, the teacher makes lesson plans to address the task and list.

  For example, if the task asks for a drawing and the assessment list asks the student to use strong, bold, bright colors to help show the brave thing that Max did, then the teacher would plan lessons to teach the student about using color to emphasize information in a drawing. The teacher would compare and contrast an example of the excellent use of color and an example of student work where color was not well-used.

  This use of drawing and color would provide an excellent opportunity for collaboration between the classroom teacher and the art teacher.

Introducing the Book in a Whole Class Group

- Take a "picture walk" through the book—look at and talk about the pictures without reading the text. (Sometimes the picture-walk is taken after the first reading of the story.)
- Read the story two or three times.
- Find pictures that show how the author used color to provide emphasis.
- During the reading, focus the students on the story line by asking them to review what has happened and predict what will happen next.
- Ask questions according to the four levels of comprehension:

Initial Understanding: describe, list, sequence, and others
Developing an Interpretation: infer, predict, generalize, etc.
Making Connections: compare, contrast, generalize, and others
Critical Stance: judge, evaluate, and others

- During the reading, focus the students on the drawings by asking them what is happening in the pictures.

Introducing the Performance Task in a Whole Class Group

- ◆ If the students are nonreaders, they will not get individual copies of the performance task page. If the students are readers, you may give each student a copy of the performance task or use a large-size version of the task page to share with the whole group.

- ◆ As a whole class group, the teacher reads the task one part at a time.

- ◆ Read the performance task again, discuss each part, and ask if there are any questions.

- ◆ Check for understanding of what the performance task is asking the students to do by asking individuals in the whole group to repeat the work to be done.

- ◆ The directions for what the students are to do are in two places. The "Procedure" part of the performance task lists the general sequence of activities. The assessment list actually provides more explicit information as to what is expected of the students. The performance task in Figure 4.9 asks for a drawing and the assessment list in Figure 4.10 asks the students to use details in the drawing. The statement of procedure in that performance task does not address "using details." It is important to keep the directions as part of the performance task brief and use the assessment list to make the expectations more explicit. The performance task asks for a drawing and the assessment list addresses how the quality of the drawing will be assessed. In this way, the student learns to depend on the assessment list.

Introducing the Assessment List in a Whole Class Group

- ◆ The assessment list is presented in a big chart form in a sentence strip holder.

- ◆ Review what the faces and Terrific, Okay, and Needs Work means. Ask the students to explain what each face means.

- ◆ Go through each element of the list—one element at a time.

- ◆ Discuss each element. For items with which the students are very familiar (Sure Things) the discussion is brief. For items on the list that are less familiar (Challenges) the teacher will need to explain what that element is about by referring to the book and/or showing models of student work. Only one item should be a Challenge on any one assessment list for primary-age students.

- ◆ The large assessment list remains posted for all to see. One copy of the assessment list may be put on the table so that the students who want to refer to it can.

Work as Individuals

- Students go to their own tables or desks to do the work. Students are seated at their tables or desks in mixed-ability groups.
- A copy of the book should be available to each group of students so that the students may refer to it anytime they need.
- Students use their quiet group voice to ask each other questions and to talk about what they are doing.

While the Students Are Drawing

- The teacher carries a copy of the assessment list as he or she walks around the room to see that all students are engaged.
- If a student is off task, talk with the student to clarify the task and then give the student a choice to continue with the work (drawing in this case) or to start over.
- As needed, talk with a student about one item on the assessment list. Focus the student on the specific part of his or her work relevant to the item on the assessment list in question.
- For the students who finish first, ask them to look at their work in relation to one item on the assessment list specified by the teacher. The teacher selects the item based on what he or she sees in the student's work.

When the Drawings Are Finished, but before the Oral Presentations

- Now each student gets an assessment list for the drawing.
- The teacher guides the class in looking at one item on the assessment list at a time. The teacher reads the assessment list item and asks the students to look at their own work and make a decision as to whether it is Terrific, Okay, or Needs Work. The student colors in the appropriate face.
- Finish the list, one item at a time.
- Do not start the oral presentations on the same day.

The Oral Presentations

- Each student brings his or her drawing back to the whole class group meeting.
- The assessment list for the oral presentation is a poster format large enough for all to see.

- The teacher reads each item on the assessment list and the class discusses what it means. The teacher may ask students to model certain behaviors such as using as a loud, large group voice.
- The teacher restates the task such as, "Show your drawing and explain how it shows that Max was a brave person."
- Each student presents his or her drawing and gives the explanation.
- Although it could be, assessment is not done on each individual student.
- Assessment is done after every one is finished presenting and explaining his or her drawing.
- An assessment list for oral presentations can focus on using a loud, sharing voice, staying on the topic, providing three examples, or using descriptive language.
- The teacher leads a discussion with the whole class as to how "we" did on each item on the assessment list. Item by item, the class decides if "we" were Terrific, Okay, or Needs Work.
- The teacher leads a discussion on what "we" could do better next time.
- The students turn in their drawings and the assessment list. (Students did not use an individual assessment list for their oral presentation.)

Final Steps

- The teacher reviews the student individual drawing and self-assessment of that drawing.
- The teacher writes comments next to each item on each assessment list as to whether the teacher agrees with the self-assessment. When there is agreement, the teacher might write, "I agree." When there is a difference of opinion between the student and the teacher on an item in the assessment list, the teacher might write, "I disagree." The teacher also says why.
- The teacher decides which students need individual discussions regarding specific items on their assessment lists.
- As needed, and on an individual basis, the teacher talks with the student to help him or her pick one way to be better next time. This process must be supportive and positive and sensitive to the developmental level of students.
- The students' work is sent to its intended audience if the task was an authentic performance task.
- Plan next steps. Here the teacher reflects on the strengths, and this may include changing the wording of assessment list items. For ex-

ample, the assessment list in Figure 4.16 states, "Did I use bright colors to show how I was brave?" The next assessment list for a drawing might reword this statement to become, "Did I use colors to show how character X was brave?" Here the teacher had decided that the students knew that the phrase "use colors" meant "use strong, bold, bright colors" so the revised assessment list item was helping to make the students more responsible and independent in understanding what was expected of them.

Later on, assessment lists for drawings might address the issue of using color by stating, "Did I use color well?" The teacher decides how quickly to revise assessment list items from very specific and explicit statements to more general statements.

Glossary of Terms

Authentic Performance Task: When the work the students do during a performance task is intended to be for an audience outside of the classroom, such as the school principal, a parent or grandparent, a student in another school, the mayor, or an author, the performance task is said to be authentic. Students are doing work that is just like work in the larger world.

Looking-Ahead Planning: This is a strategy of selecting the performance task to be used in a unit of instruction well in advance of getting into that unit. Once the performance task has been selected, the teacher studies the task and its assessment list to focus on the content and process skills important to students' success. The teacher pays particular attention to the challenging aspects of the new task and its assessment list and then plans instruction to teach the important content and/or process skills.

Performance Task: A performance task is both a learning activity and an opportunity to assess student performance. In the area of reading comprehension, a performance task asks the student to do something such as describe and sequence (Initial Understanding), make and support inferences (Developing an Interpretation), compare and contrast (Making Connections), and judge and evaluate (Critical Stance). In the primary grades, a performance task is limited to one such task.

Simulated Authentic Performance Task: When the audience for the student's work is really not going to get the work, then the performance task is a simulated authentic performance task. During a simulated authentic performance task, the students may be pretending to write to the President or a Disney Studios movie director, or George Washington, or a character in a book. Both authentic and simulated authentic performance tasks put the student in the role of communicating with a person other than the classroom teacher or the fellow classmates.

References

Falwell, C. (2001). *David's drawings.* New York: Lee and Low Books.

Being Brave

Brave Bear and the Ghosts: A Sioux legend. (1996). (Retold by G. Dominic; C. Reasoner, Illus.). Troll Communications.

Chapouton, A. (1986). *Billy the Brave* (J. Claverie, Illus.). New York: Holt Rinehart and Winston.

Mayer, M. (1968). *There's Something There!* New York: Penguin Putnam.

O'Connor, J. (1990). *Molly the brave* (S. Hamanaka, Illus.). New York: Random House. Muir, J. (1998) *Stricken* (Retold by D. Ruba; C. Canyon, Illus.). Nevada City, CA: Dawn Publications.

Sendak, M. (1963). *Where The Wild Things Are.* New York: HarperCollins.

Steig, W. (1986). *Brave Irene.* Farrar, Straus, and Giroux.

Williams, L. (1986). *The Little Old Lady Who Was Not Afraid Of Anything* (M. Lloyd, Illus.). New York, HarperCollins.

5

Teaching and Assessing Reading Comprehension of Nonfiction through Drawing

Topics in This Chapter

♦ Strategies for using a framework for reading comprehension that focuses on thinking-skill verbs to make performance tasks, asking students to draw and present orally.

♦ Strategies to make analytic rubrics, holistic rubrics, and assessment lists for judging the quality of drawings and oral presentations.

♦ Strategies to use performance tasks and assessment tools in the context of language arts or another discipline.

Four Levels of Comprehension

The four levels of comprehension: *Initial Understanding*, *Developing an Interpretation*, *Making Connections*, and *Critical Stance* are defined in Chapter 4. Chapter 5 expands that definition, and Figure 5.1 presents a collection of some of the verbs that are used with each of the four levels of comprehension.

Attention to Details through Drawing

The accurate reporting of showing details through drawing is a form of Initial Understanding. When students are asked to "draw a picture of a human skeleton," they may or may not pay attention to the details. But when the assignment is to pay attention to the details of the bones in the hand, and the preceding lessons have shown what it looks like when drawings show the details, the student's attention and drawings are much more precise. This attention to detail is the basis for the other levels of understanding that require the student to carry out such processes as inferring, comparing, contrasting, categorizing, or evaluating.

During a unit on skeletons, to show Initial Understanding, a student may be asked to illustrate a skeleton (drawing) and describe (oral presentation in this chapter and writing in following chapters) five bones in the drawing. To show Developing an Interpretation, the student may be asked to compare the bones in the leg with the bones in the arm. To show Making Connections, the student may be asked to compare the bones in a human arm with the bones in a bird's wing. To show Critical Stance, the student may be asked to judge which picture of a skeleton is the best one to teach about bones. A unit on the skeleton would involve students in all four levels of comprehension. One particular performance task would engage primary-age students in only one of the levels of comprehension. It would take a series of tasks to cover all four levels of comprehension.

Figure 5.1. Verbs Used For Each of Four Levels of Comprehension

Level of Understanding	Verbs Used to Direct Thinking
Initial Understanding (i.e., Literal understanding)	Describe, Display, Illustrate, Label, Locate, List, Sequence, Show, Summarize
Developing an Interpretation (Based on using one source of information, i.e., one book.)	Categorize, Compare, Conclude, Contrast, Design, Estimate, Explain, Generalize, Infer, Interpret, Predict, Support
Making Connections (Based on using **two or more** information sources, i.e., two books or one book and a hands-on activity.)	Categorize, Compare, Conclude, Contrast, Design, Estimate, Explain, Generalize, Infer, Interpret, Predict, Support
Critical Stance (Judging the accuracy and quality of information from one source.)	Evaluate, Judge, Rank, Rate

Principles and Elements of Design

The Principles and Elements of Design were presented and defined in Chapter 4. Figure 5.2 presents a chart used for planning which Principles and Elements will be used in specific performance tasks requiring students to make drawings. Collaboration with an art teacher is helpful in this process.

Figure 5.2. Principles and Elements of Design: Used to Help the Observer/Artist Convey Information

Principles of Design	Elements of Design Used to Accomplish Principles						
	Texture	Shape	Form	Line	Color	Value	Space
Pattern							
Move-ment							
Balance							
Unity							
Contrast							
Rhythm							
Emphasis		X		X	X		X

Drawings for the tasks about skeletons in this chapter require the student to draw accurate patterns of the bones and the unity of the whole skeleton. "Pattern" and "Unity" are two Principles of Design. The Element of Design, "Shape," is very important to accomplishing the purposes of drawings of skeletons. So, tasks about drawing skeletons would emphasize accurate use of shapes to show the pattern of bones in the whole skeleton.

Drawings for tasks about the solar system in this chapter require the student to draw the planets so that descriptions and comparisons can be made. The Principles of "Pattern" and "Emphasis" are important, and the student will accomplish them through the use of "Shape," "Form," "Color," and "Value."

Drawings for the tasks about dinosaurs in this chapter will focus on the use of color and details of shape and form to emphasize the content of the drawing, i.e., show how the dinosaur uses its body parts to get and eat its food. Figure 5.2 has been marked to show how the teacher planning the tasks about the dinosaurs used this chart.

Analytic Rubric for Drawings and Oral Presentations Based on Nonfiction

For each item on an assessment list, the teachers and students must understand what "Terrific," "Okay," and "Needs Work" mean. Writing the descriptions for each of those three levels of performance in the analytic rubric helps the teacher understand more clearly what those three levels mean.

Examples of student work are used in conjunction with the analytic rubric to more clearly define the levels of performance. The teacher collects student work samples that show what "Terrific" looks like (drawings) or sounds like (video tape of oral presentations) for each of the specific behaviors in the analytic rubric. Other samples of student work or performance can be collected to show the "Okay" and "Needs Work" levels of performance.

Analytic Rubric For Drawing

The analytic rubric in Figure 5.3 is similar to the rubric for drawing in Figure 4.2, but the rubric in this chapter make more use of the Principles and Elements of Design.

Figure 5.3. Analytic Rubric for Drawing

Specific Behavior	Levels of Performance		
	3: Terrific	2: Okay	1: Needs Work
On the topic	The drawing is clearly and entirely on the topic of the assignment.	The drawing is on the topic but may have "strayed off-topic" a little.	The drawing is off the topic.
Shows details	Just the right amount of accurate details of shape, form and color are used. The details are just the right ones to respond to the thinking-skill verb for the task. For example, if the task calls for a comparison, the drawing shows the details important to making the comparison.	Either a few too many or too many details are used. There may be a few minor inaccuracies. The details provided are relevant to the thinking-skill verb for the task.	There are no details, or there are major inaccuracies in the details. The details are not particularly relevant to the thinking skill verb for the task.
Uses proportions	The proportions are correct.	The proportions are nearly correct.	The elements in the drawing are totally out of proportion.
Accomplishes emphasis	Strong emphasis is accomplished on the parts of the drawing that should be emphasized. Elements such as color, value, texture, and shape help to provide this emphasis.	Appropriate emphasis is made, although it is not quite strong enough.	Emphasis is not made, or it is made on inappropriate elements of the drawing.
Shows patterns	The patterns that are relevant to the topic are shown very well. Elements such as color and shape help to create the pattern.	The patterns are shown, but they could be more pronounced.	The patterns that are to be shown are not.

Shows contrasts	Contrasts are used very well to help emphasize the content of the drawing, especially when the thinking-skill verbs are "compare and contrast."	Contrasts are made appropriate to the assignment.	Contrasts are not made.
Uses foreground, middleground, and background	The drawing clearly uses foreground, middleground, and background.	The student uses only two of these levels, such as foreground and background.	Only one level is used.
Uses paper	Uses the entire paper well.	Uses most of the paper well.	Does not use the paper well.
Is neat	Is very neat	Is neat	Is not neat
Overall impact	The drawing makes a very strong impression and captures the attention of the audience.	The drawing makes an impression and captures some attention from the audience.	The drawing makes little impression and captures little, if any, attention.

Analytic Rubric for Oral Presentation

The analytic rubric in Figure 5.4 is similar to the analytic rubric for oral presentation shown in Figure 4.3. The rubric in this chapter places greater emphasis on the degree to which the student provides information according to the thinking-skill verb for the task. For example, if the thinking-skill verb is "compare and contrast," the student is expected to provide a specific number of examples to make the comparisons and a specified number of examples to make the contrasts.

Figure 5.4. Analytic Rubric for Oral Presentations About Drawings

Specific Behavior	*Levels of Performance*		
	3: Terrific	**2: Okay**	**1: Needs Work**
On the topic	The presentation is entirely on the topic of the assignment. The student very clearly answers the question about the drawing.	Most of the presentation is about the drawing. The student answers questions about the drawing.	The student strays off-topic often.
Presents the drawing	The student shows the drawing for all to see clearly. The student may show the drawing several times as needed in the oral presentation.	The student shows the drawing for most to see clearly.	The drawing is not presented well—not many students can see it.
Presents information relevant to the thinking-skill verb for the task.	The student provides sufficient accurate examples to accomplish the purpose of the task, i.e., describe, compare/contrast, infer, evaluate, or judge.	The student provides some accurate examples to accomplish the purpose of the task.	The details are lacking, or they do not respond to the purpose of the task, i.e., the student may simply describe, rather than compare and contrast.
Uses descriptive language	The student uses the vocabulary of the topic and other descriptive language very well.	The student uses the vocabulary of the topic and other descriptive language.	The student uses few, if any, of the vocabulary of the topic and little other descriptive language.
Uses a loud, group-sharing voice	The student uses a loud, group-sharing voice throughout the presentation.	The student uses a loud, group-sharing for most of the presentation.	The student's voice is too soft most, or all, of the time.

Holistic Rubrics for Drawings and Oral Presentations

A holistic rubric is used to describe the overall quality of a student's work or performance. Here, the holistic rubric shows four levels of performance: "Above Goal," "At Goal," "Near Goal," and "Below Goal." The "Goal" refers to the level of performance that the classroom teacher or school or school district sets as the standard to meet. If you were to assign a "report card grade" to the level titled "At Goal" it would be about a B or B+. Work better than that is "Above Goal," work almost as good as "At Goal" is called "Near Goal," and work very inferior to "At Goal" is called "Below Goal."

It is essential that examples of student work be selected that show what it "looks like or sounds like" "Above Goal," "At Goal," "Near Goal," and "Below Goal." The holistic rubric and the examples of student work together define what is meant by each of these four levels of performance. Models of excellent drawings would be the drawings themselves. Models of excellent oral presentations would be oral presentations on video tapes.

The teacher can use the holistic rubric within a grade to track the progress towards, and even beyond, the goal. "At Goal" drawings and oral presentations in grade one would be of less quality than "At Goal" work in an upper grade. The same holistic rubric can be used for a sequence of grade levels, but the student work serving as examples for each of the levels within the holistic rubric must be appropriate to each grade level in that sequence. A student "At Goal" in grade one and still "At Goal" in grade three would have made much progress because the standards of excellence to be "At Goal" in grade three are much higher than in grade one.

One problem with holistic rubrics is that they may not be able to show why a student is "overall" near goal. There are many reasons that the student's work may be described as only "Near Goal." For example, the work of one student may be Near Goal because proportions are not used well enough, whereas the work of another student may be Near Goal because foregound/middleground/background are not used well enough. The holistic "score" does not give the teacher or student precise information about specific strengths and needs of individual students. The use of analytic rubrics and holistic rubrics to help generate assessment lists is discussed later in this chapter.

Figure 5.5. Holistic Rubric for Drawings

Level of Performance	Description of the Level of Performance
Above Goal	The student's drawing is completely on the topic of the assignment and uses many accurate details. The student also uses proportion very accurately; uses foreground, middleground, and background well; uses elements of design very well as called for in the assignment; uses all of the paper; and is very neat.
At Goal	The student's drawing is on the topic of the assignment and uses several accurate details. The student uses most of the following areas such as: uses proportion mostly accurately; uses foreground, middleground, and background; uses elements of design well as called for in the assignment; uses most of the paper; and is neat.
Near Goal	The student's drawing is mostly on the topic and uses a few accurate details. There is a significant shortcoming in two or more areas such as: use of proportion; use of foreground, middleground, and background; or elements of design required by the assignment.
Below Goal	The student's drawing is not on the topic and/or uses inaccurate details. There are many shortcomings in areas such as the use of proportion, elements of design, use of paper space, and neatness.

Figure 5.6. Holistic Rubric for Oral Presentations

Level of Performance	Description of the Level of Performance
Above Goal	The student displays the drawing very clearly to everyone and as often as necessary. The student uses a loud, group-sharing voice throughout the presentation. The student provides accurate information on the topic and according to the thinking-skill verb for this task, i.e., the student provides information to both compare and contrast if the task calls for those thinking skills. The student uses excellent descriptive language and vocabulary appropriate to the topic.
At Goal	The student displays the drawing clearly to everyone. The student uses a loud, group-sharing voice most of the time in the presentation. The student provides accurate information on the topic and according to the thinking-skill verb for this task, i.e., the student provides information to both compare and contrast if the task calls for those thinking skills. The level of detail is satisfactory but not at the excellent level. The student uses descriptive language and some vocabulary appropriate to the topic.
Near Goal	The student does not display the drawing clearly enough. The student's voice is too soft. The student provides some information on the topic but some may be inaccurate, i.e., the task may require three details and the student only provides one. The student does not completely respond to the requirement of the thinking-skill verb, i.e., the student provides information about the similarities of two things when the thinking skill calls for both similarities and differences. The student uses little descriptive language and/or vocabulary specific to the topic.
Below Goal	The student displays the drawing poorly and uses a voice that is much too soft. The information in the presentation is off topic, inaccurate, and/or insufficient in quantity. The student does not provide information according to the thinking-skill verb, i.e., the student may only describe one item rather than comparing and contrasting it with another item.

Making Performance Tasks

Drawing provides the information needed in the oral presentation. When the overall task is to describe, the drawing presents the information that is pointed to during the oral description. Likewise, if the overall task is to compare two skeletons, the drawing provides the accurate details and the comparison is made in the oral presentation. The tasks in this chapter require both drawing and oral presentation.

Developing Ideas for Performance Tasks

Making a chart of ideas helps ensure that the overall collection of performance tasks addresses all four levels of comprehension. For primary age students, performance tasks address only one level of comprehension, so a set of tasks is required to address the four levels of comprehension. Figure 5.7 presents four tasks for each of three content topics—skeletons, the solar system, and dinosaurs.

Creating a chart of ideas for performance tasks in each of the four levels of comprehension also help avoid two common problems of creating sets of performance tasks. The first problem is the tendency to make too many tasks at the Initial Understanding level. The second problem is to have too few tasks at the Critical Stance level. A balance of all four levels is desirable.

Figure 5.7. Ideas for Performance Tasks

Book Title	Level of Comprehension	Ideas for Performance Tasks
SKELETON Plastic models of skeletons, Xrays, and bones from chicken skeletons, in addition to books, would enrich these lessons		
The Skeleton Inside You or any book with a good drawing of the front view of a human skeleton.	IU	Draw a picture of the human skeleton. **Describe** orally.
Skeletons or any book with a good drawing of the bones in the human hand.	DI	Draw a picture of your hand showing the bones inside your hand. **Conclude** orally.
Rattle Your Bones for the human skeleton. *Dinosaur Skeletons and other Prehistoric Animals* *Visual Dictionary of the Skeleton* for the skeletons of a variety of humans and a variety of other animals.	MC	Draw a picture of a human skeleton and a picture of a skeleton of another kind of animal. Find two ways the skeletons are the same and two ways they are different. **Compare** and **contrast** orally.
All the books you have in your classroom with pictures of human skeletons.	CS	Find the best picture (drawing) of a skeleton (any kind of skeleton) in one of your books and copy that picture (drawing.) **Evaluate** orally.
SOLAR SYSTEM Posters of photographs of objects in the solar system and models of the solar system would enrich these lessons.		
The Sun's Family of Planets or any other book with photographs of the planets. Use photographs rather than drawings for this task.	IU	Draw a picture of your favorite planet other than Earth. **Describe** orally.

The Magic School Bus Lost in the Solar System or another book that shows photographs and or drawings of planets, moons, the sun, comets, asteroids, and other objects in our solar system.	DI	Draw a picture of something in the solar system that is not a planet. **Categorize** orally.
Me and My Place in Space and *The Sun's Family of Planets* and any other books that show photographs or realistic drawings of the Earth and other planets.	MC	Draw a picture of the Earth and another planet. **Compare** and **contrast** orally.
The Magic School Bus Lost in the Solar System	CS	Draw a picture of one thing in The Magic School Bus Lost in the Solar System that is fantasy. **Judge** orally.
DINOSAURS Posters of dinosaurs, plastic models, and videos of dinosaurs would enrich these lessons.		
How Big Is A Brachiosaurus? or any other book that has good pictures of dinosaurs.	IU	Draw a picture of your favorite dinosaur. **Describe** orally.
Dinosaur Skeletons and Other Prehistoric Animals or any other book that has good pictures of the body parts important to getting and eating food. Present both meat eating and plant eating dinosaurs.	DI	Draw a picture of a dinosaur that shows how it uses its body parts to help it get food and eat it. **Explain** orally.
Did Comets Kill the Dinosaurs?	MC	Draw a picture that explains why there are no dinosaurs around today. **Infer** orally.
All the books in your room about dinosaurs.	CS	Draw a picture from the book that you thought was the most factual book about dinosaurs. **Rate** orally.

IU = Initial Understanding, DI = Developing an Interpretation, MC = Making Connections,
CS = Critical Stance

Creating the Performance Task

Once ideas have been generated for performance tasks they can be engineered into actual performance tasks for students. Consider the idea for the performance task that states, "Draw a picture from the book that you thought was the most factual book about dinosaurs." This is a "Critical Stance" task because the student is being asked to rate the books based on the degree to which they present factual information rather than fictionalized accounts of dinosaurs.

Figure 5.30 presents the final version of the completed performance task.

♦ All of the narrative in the task is written "**to the student.**"

♦ The **Background** sets the stage for the task. In this task the students are reminded that they have read both factual books about dinosaurs and books that were fantasies. The Background is kept short.

♦ The **Task** tells the student exactly what he or she is to make or do in the performance task.

♦ The section of the task entitled, "**Audience,**" explains for whom the work is intended. In this task, the student's opinion as to the best book is intended for the classroom teacher. Audiences in other tasks include older students, library media teachers, book authors, illustrators, parents, and space tourists. Authentic tasks have real audiences and simulated authentic tasks have simulated audiences.

♦ The section of the task entitled, "**Purpose,**" explains why the student is doing this work for the specified audience. In this case, the purpose of the student's work is to persuade the teacher to buy a specific book for the classroom library.

♦ The **Procedure** presents a short, simple list of the steps in the performance task. The assessment lists will focus the students on how to pay attention to the quality of their work. The Procedure is like a checklist of what to do, and the assessment list addresses the quality of the work.

♦ The whole performance task is one page long.

Making Assessment Lists for the Performance Tasks

The following are some guidelines for making assessment lists for specific performance tasks. Chapter 4 presents guidelines that are summarized here.

♦ **The purpose of an assessment list is to get the students to pay attention to as much as they will pay attention to.** So, the number of items and the wording of each item must be appropriate to this purpose.

♦ **Create only the number of items the students can handle.**

- **Be sure that some items are clearly related to the content of the performance task**. Item number one in Figure 5.9 and item number three in Figure 5.10 address the content of the task to draw and describe the skeleton.

- **Create some items about the use of process skills.** Items number two and three in Figure 5.22 address the use of color and shape in the drawing to help make the comparisons of Earth and another planet.

- **Use the analytic rubric to generate items**. One specific behavior in the analytic rubric in Figure 5.3 is "Accomplishes Emphasis" and the descriptors of the "Terrific" level of performance states that color, value, and texture are important in creating emphasis. So, items in assessment lists where emphasis is important include items such as, "Did I use colors to make my dinosaur stand out?" (Figure 5.26)

- **Use the principles and elements of design to generate items**. Figure 5.2 presents the Principles and Elements of Design, and it shows how one teacher has selected the elements of shape, form, color, and value to accomplish the Principles of pattern and emphasis in the drawing of the solar system. Item number 3 in Figure 5.18 asks, "Did I use circles correctly?" in reference to drawings of a planet other than the Earth.

- **"Sure Thing" items**. Some items must be about what the students will find easy to do because of their knowledge and skills. Item number one in Figure 5.28 asks, "Did I draw a dinosaur getting and eating its food?" is probably a "sure thing" type of item.

- **"Challenge" items**. One item (in assessment lists longer than one item) on the assessment list should be a challenge for the students. Item number two in Figure 5.21 asks, "Did I use details to show how the dinosaurs used its body parts to get and eat food?" Answering this involves a complicated task. The teacher needs to spend class time before this performance task is introduced to teach students how to "see" and draw how animals use their mouths, teeth, and limbs to get and eat food.

- **The specificity of items**. Challenge items must be stated in very detailed and specific terms. Item number three in Figure 5.30 asks, "Did I use color to emphasize what happened?" This is less specific than asking, "Did I use color to emphasize what happened to make all the dinosaurs disappear?" and more specific than asking, "Did I use color well?" The teacher decides how specific to make the item. Inexperienced students need very specific items. As the students get more experience, more responsibility should be placed on them to "understand" what an assessment list item means.

When an experienced student sees the assessment list item, "Did I use color well?," he or she expands that statement in his or her head to become, "Did I use the appropriate colors in the right intensity to emphasize the particular part of the picture that I want to stand out to my audience?" The long-term goal of using assessment lists is to help students create assessment lists in their heads and no longer need assessment lists from teachers. That long-term goal can be met after years of experience with assessment lists.

♦ **Put items in question format**. Questions direct learning.

♦ **Simple versus complex items**. A simple item in an assessment list involves only one direction, and a complex item involves two or more to do. Items number one and two in Figure 5.18 are simple items. A more experienced student could handle a more complex item such as, "Did I use the name of the planet and give three reasons why it is my favorite?"

♦ **Involve students in helping to create assessment lists**. The point of assessment lists is to coach students to take responsibility for assessing their own work and improving their performance. When possible, the students should be involved in conversations to create assessment lists.

After the students are experienced in using several assessment lists that are, for example, about making drawings of some aspect of stories, the teacher might work with the whole group to create an assessment list for the drawing required in the next performance task.

Assessment Lists for Drawings and for Oral Descriptions of Drawings

Each task in this chapter includes an assessment list for the student's drawing. The first task, Drawing of a Skeleton, has an assessment list for the student's oral description of the drawing. Subsequent performance tasks do not include an assessment list for oral presentations. Assessment lists can be used, or a sentence strip chart can be made to be used, for all oral presentations.

Figure 5.8a. Performance Task:
Drawing of a Skeleton
see the assessment lists on pages 94 and 95

Background
There are many bones in a human skeleton. The bones in the skeletons of boys and girls are growing and we need to take good care of our skeletons.
Task
Your task is to draw a detailed picture of the human skeleton.
Audience
Your pictures are for the school nurse.
Purpose
The nurse will exhibit your drawings in her office to help remind all the boys and girls in the school to take care of their skeletons.
Procedure
1. Study pictures of the human skeleton.
2. Make a detailed drawing of the human skeleton.
3. Check your drawing to make sure you have drawn all the bones.

Figure 5.9a. Performance Task:
Bones in My Hand
see the assessment list on page 96

Background
Look at your hand and move your fingers. Feel your fingers and hand with your other hand. What is inside your hand under your skin?
Task
Your task is to draw the bones in your hand.
Audience
The other students in your school will see your drawings.
Purpose
You will display your bony hands so the other students will have fun looking at them.
Procedure
1. Put your hand down flat on a piece of paper.
2. Trace the outline of your hand.
3. Draw the bones in your fingers and palm of your hand.
4. Cut out the drawing of your hand.
5. Tape your cutout on the display area.

Figure 5.8b. Performance Task Assessment List: Drawing of a Skeleton

1. Did I draw the human skeleton?

Terrific   OK   Needs Work

2. Did I show many details of the skeleton?

Terrific   OK   Needs Work

3. Did I use the right shapes for the bones?

Terrific   OK   Needs Work

4. Is my work neat?

Terrific   OK   Needs Work

Figure 5.8c. Performance Task Assessment List: Drawing of a Skeleton (Oral Presentation)

1. Did I show my drawing so that everyone could see it?

Terrific   OK   Needs Work

2. Did I speak in my loud, group sharing voice?

Terrific   OK   Needs Work

3.Did I describe at least five bones in my drawing?

Terrific   OK   Needs Work

Figure 5.9b. Performance Task Assessment List: Bones in My Hand (Drawing)

1. Did I check the book and the model skeleton of a hand?

Terrific   OK   Needs Work

2. Did I draw the details of the bones in my fingers and palm?

Terrific   OK   Needs Work

3. Did I draw the correct shapes for the bones?

Terrific   OK   Needs Work

4. Did I check my work?

Terrific   OK   Needs Work

Figure 5.10a. Performance Task:
Bones in Birds and Me
see the assessment list on page 98

Background
Many kinds of animals have skeletons inside of them. These skeletons are like our skeletons in some ways. These skeletons are different from our skeletons in other ways.

Task
You will draw a picture with two parts. One part will be a picture of a human skeleton. The second part will be a picture of a bird skeleton.

Audience
The nature center would like to display your pictures.

Purpose
Your pictures will teach people about how bird and human skeletons are the same and different.

Procedure
1. Draw the human skeleton.
2. Draw the bird skeleton.
3. Use the assessment list to check your work.

Figure 5.11a. Performance Task:
My Favorite Skeleton Picture
see the assessment list on page 99

Background
We have seen many pictures of skeletons. Which one was your favorite? Why was it your favorite?

Task
Your task is to find your favorite picture of a skeleton and draw a copy of it.

Audience
You will send your drawing to the illustrator of the book that contains your favorite picture of a skeleton.

Purpose
By sending your drawings to the illustrator, you will be telling the illustrator that you liked the drawing they made.

Procedure
1. Find your favorite picture of a skeleton.
2. Draw it.
3. Use the assessment list to check your work.

Figure 5.10b. Performance Task Assessment List:
Bones in Birds and Me (Drawing)

1. Did I make a detailed drawing of the human skeleton?

Terrific   OK   Needs Work

2. Did I make a detailed drawing of a bird skeleton?

Terrific   OK   Needs Work

3. Did I use the correct shapes for the bones in each skeleton?

Terrific   OK   Needs Work

4. Is my work neat?

Terrific   OK   Needs Work

Figure 5.11b. Performance Task Assessment List: My Favorite Skeleton Picture (Drawing)

1. Did I draw a copy of my favorite skeleton picture?

| Terrific | OK | Needs Work |

2. Did I copy the picture correctly?

| Terrific | OK | Needs Work |

3. Did I draw a star next to my favorite part of the picture?

| Terrific | OK | Needs Work |

4. Is my work neat?

| Terrific | OK | Needs Work |

Figure 5.12a. Performance Task:
My Favorite Other Planet
see the assessment list on page 101

Background
In addition to Earth, there are eight planets in our solar system. Which other planet is your favorite?

Task
Your task is to draw a very interesting picture of your favorite other planet. (Do not draw the Earth.)

Audience
Pretend that you are a travel agent talking to people about traveling to your favorite planet.

Purpose
You want to convince other people to travel to your favorite other planet.

Procedure
1. Pick your favorite other planet.
2. Draw a picture of how that planet looks from a spaceship.
3. Use the assessment list to check your work.

Figure 5.13a. Performance Task:
A Tour of Our Solar System
see the assessment list on page 102

Background
There are nine planets in our solar system. There are many other kinds of things in our solar system also. What are the other things in our solar system?

Task
Your job is to pick one thing in our solar system that is not a planet and draw a picture of it.

Audience
The parents who are coming to an open house at our school will see your drawings of all the amazing things in our solar system.

Purpose
Your drawings will show the parents all about the different kinds of things in our solar system.

Procedure
1. Select one thing to draw that is not a planet.
2. Draw a picture of that interesting thing.
3. Use the assessment list to check your work.

Figure 5.12b. Performance Task Assessment List:
My Favorite Other Planet (Drawing)

1. Did I draw a picture of my favorite other planet?

Terrific   OK   Needs Work

2. Did I use color to make my drawing interesting?

Terrific   OK   Needs Work

3. Did I use circles correctly?

Terrific   OK   Needs Work

4. Is my work neat?

Terrific   OK   Needs Work

Figure 5.13b. Performance Task Assessment List:
A Tour of Our Solar System (Drawing)

1. Did I draw something in our solar system that is not a planet?

Terrific   OK   Needs Work

2. Did I use colors to make my drawing interesting?

Terrific   OK   Needs Work

3. Did I use at least three different shapes in my drawing?

Terrific   OK   Needs Work

4. Is my work neat?

Terrific   OK   Needs Work

Figure 5.14a. Performance Task: How Is the Earth the Same and Different from Other Planets?
see the assessment list on page 104

Background
There are nine planets in our solar system. Each one is very different from the others. All of the other planets are very different from the Earth.

Task
Your job is to draw a picture of the Earth and one other planet to show how they are the same and how they are different.

Audience
You will send your pictures to the students who study space at the high school.

Purpose
Your pictures will show the high school students what you are learning about planets.

Procedure
1. Draw a picture of the Earth.
2. Draw a picture of one other planet.
3. Use the assessment list to check your work.

Figure 5.15a. Performance Task: Real and Fantasy about Space
see the assessment list on page 105

Background
The book, *The Magic School Bus Lost in Space*, is a very interesting story. Some of the things that happen in that story are fantasy.

Task
Draw a picture of one thing that is a fantasy in the story.

Audience
The library teacher is making a display called *Fantasy* and the *Truth*. The library teacher will use your pictures to show how books about real things sometimes have fantasy in them also.

Purpose
The purpose of your drawing of a fantasy is to help the library teacher explain the difference between *Fantasy* and the *Truth*.

Procedure
1. Select a fantasy from the story.
2. Draw a picture of the fantasy.
3. Use your assessment list to check your work.

Figure 5.14b. Performance Task Assessment List: How Is the Earth the Same and Different from Other Planets? (Drawing)

1. Did I draw the Earth and one other planet?

2. Did I use color to show the differences between the Earth and the other planet?

3. Did I use shapes to show differences between the Earth and the other planet?

4. Is my work neat?

Figure 5.15b. Performance Task Assessment List: Real and Fantasy about Space (Drawing)

1. Did I draw a picture of a fantasy from the story?

Terrific	OK	Needs Work

2. Did I draw many details of the fantasy?

Terrific	OK	Needs Work

3. Did I use color to make my drawing interesting?

Terrific	OK	Needs Work

4. Did I use shapes to make my drawing interesting?

Terrific	OK	Needs Work

Figure 5.16a. Performance Task:
An Amazing Dinosaur!
see the assessment list on page 107

Background
Dinosaurs were amazing animals. Which dinosaur was the most amazing to you?

Task
Draw a picture of your favorite dinosaur.

Audience
Children in another school are studying dinosaurs and you will send your pictures to them.

Purpose
Your pictures will show them which dinosaurs are our favorites.

Procedure
1. Select your favorite dinosaur.
2. Draw a picture of your favorite dinosaur.
3. Show the dinosaur living in its home.
4. Use the assessment list to check your work.

Figure 5.17a. Performance Task:
Dinner Time for Dinosaurs
see the assessment list on page 108

Background
All animals need to eat to stay alive. Each type of dinosaur ate a certain kind of food. Dinosaurs had body parts that helped them find, get, and eat food.

Task
You will draw a picture of a dinosaur that shows exactly how it used its body parts to find, get, and eat food.

Audience
You will put your pictures in the cafeteria where boys and girls line up to get their lunch.

Purpose
Your drawings will be interesting and they will show how dinosaurs got their dinner.

Procedure
1. Select a dinosaur that you know about. You must know what that dinosaur ate.
2. Draw a picture of that dinosaur. Show how it found, got, and ate its food.
3. Use the assessment list to check your work.

Figure 5.16b. Performance Task Assessment List: An Amazing Dinosaur! (Drawing)

1. Did I draw my favorite dinosaur living in its home?

Terrific   OK   Needs Work

2. Did I use colors to make my dinosaur stand out?

Terrific   OK   Needs Work

3. Did I use foreground, middleground, and background?

Terrific   OK   Needs Work

4. Did I use many details in the picture?

Terrific   OK   Needs Work

5. Is my work neat?

Terrific   OK   Needs Work

Figure 5.17b. Performance Task Assessment List: Dinner Time for Dinosaurs (Drawing)

1. Did I draw a dinosaur getting and eating its food?

Terrific	OK	Needs Work

2. Did I use details to show how the dinosaur used its body parts to get and eat food?

Terrific	OK	Needs Work

3. Did I use color to emphasize how dinosaurs eat?

Terrific	OK	Needs Work

4. Did I use foreground, middleground, and background?

Terrific	OK	Needs Work

5. Is my work neat?

Terrific	OK	Needs Work

Figure 5.18a. Performance Task:
The Mystery of Dinosaurs
see the assessment list on page 110

Background
Many kinds of dinosaurs lived all over the earth and in the seas for millions of years. But they are all gone today. What happened?

Task
Your task is to draw a picture that shows one possible reason why the dinosaurs disappeared.

Audience
Your drawing will be used in a book called, *The Mystery of Why Dinosaurs Disappeared*. The book will be put into the library.

Purpose
The book will teach other people some ideas about what happened to the dinosaurs.

Procedure
   1.   Draw a picture that shows what happened to make the dinosaurs disappear from Earth.
   2.   Use the assessment list to check your work.

Figure 5.19a. Performance Task:
Best Factual Book about Dinosaurs
see the assessment list on page 111

Background
We have read many books about dinosaurs and seen many videos. Some of what we have seen is make-believe or fantasy. Some of what we have seen is factual.

Task
What is the best book for factual information about dinosaurs?
Your job is to select the book that you think does the best job of telling the facts. You will copy a picture from the best book.

Audience
Your teacher wants to buy more copies of the most factual book about dinosaurs. You will help your teacher make the decision about which book to buy.

Purpose
Your ideas about the best book will help your teacher decide which book to buy.

Procedure
   1.   Review the books you have used about dinosaurs.
   2.   Select the book that is the most factual.
   3.   Copy the best picture from the book that is the most factual.

Figure 5.18b. Performance Task Assessment:
The Mystery of Dinosaurs (Drawing)

1. Did I draw a picture that shows what may have happened to make the dinosaurs disappear from Earth?

      Terrific   OK   Needs Work

2. Did I show details of what happened to the dinosaurs?

      Terrific   OK   Needs Work

3. Did I use color to emphasize what happened?

      Terrific   OK   Needs Work

4. Did I use foreground, middleground, and background?

      Terrific   OK   Needs Work

5. Is my work neat?

      Terrific   OK   Needs Work

Figure 5.19b. Performance Task Assessment List: Best Factual Book about Dinosaurs (Drawing)

1. Did I pick a book that I thought gave the best facts about dinosaurs?

Terrific   OK   Needs Work

2. Did I copy a picture from that book?

Terrific   OK   Needs Work

3. Did I copy the picture correctly?

Terrific   OK   Needs Work

4. Did I put three stars next to parts of the picture that I liked the best?

Terrific   OK   Needs Work

Using Performance Tasks and Assessment Lists

Note: The steps of "Introducing the Book to the Whole Class Group" through and including "Using the Assessment List for the Drawing" are done on the same day. The oral presentation is done on the next day.

Chapter 4 presents the details of the sequence of events in a unit of instruction starting before the unit is begun and concluding with steps to take after all the work on the performance task is completed. See Chapter 4 for those details. Additional details are presented here.

Before the Book

- Work on skills regarding classroom routines, individual work habits, and group work.
- Teach to the "challenge" items in the assessment list.

Introducing the Book in a Whole Class Group

- Read the story.
- Take a "picture walk."
- Find pictures that show how the author used color to provide emphasis.
- During the reading, focus the students on the story line.
- Ask questions according to the four levels of comprehension.
- During the reading focus the student on the drawings.

Introducing the Performance Task in a Whole Class Group

- Read the task to the students.
- Reread the task with students' help.
- Check for understanding.

Introducing the Assessment List in a Whole Class Group

- Present the assessment list to the group.
- Review what the faces and Terrific, Okay, and Needs Work mean.
- Go through each element of the list—one element at a time.
- Discuss each element.
- Let students have access to the assessment list while they work.

Work as Individuals

- Students go to their own tables or desks to do the work.
- A copy of the book should be available to each group of students.
- Students use their quiet group voice to ask each other questions and to talk about what they are doing.

While the Students Are Drawing

- The teacher sees that all students are engaged.
- As needed, talk with individual students.
- Encourage students to check their work.

When the Drawings Are Finished, but before the Oral Presentations

- Each student gets an assessment list for the drawing.
- The teacher guides the class in looking at the assessment list.
- Finish the list one item at a time.
- Do not start the oral presentations on the same day.

The Oral Presentations

- Each student brings his or her drawing back to the whole class group meeting.
- The assessment list for the oral presentation is a poster format large enough for all to see.
- The teacher reads each item on the assessment list and the class discusses what it means.
- The teacher restates the task such as, "Show your drawing and explain how it compares the Earth and another planet."
- Each student presents his or her drawing and gives the explanation.
- Assessment is done after every one is finished presenting and explaining his or her drawing.
- The teacher leads a discussion with the whole class as to how "we" did on each item on the assessment list.
- The teacher leads a discussion on what we could do better next time.
- The students turn in their drawings and the assessment list that they used about the drawing

Final Step

- The teacher uses the assessment list to assess the student's work.

- The teacher talks to individuals, small groups, or the whole class about the strengths and weaknesses on the drawing and oral presentations.
- The students' work is sent to its intended audience if relevant.
- Plan how to focus on content and process skills in subsequent instruction.
- Decide what kinds of "sure thing" and "challenge" items should go on the next assessment list.

Glossary of Terms

Holistic Rubric: This type of scoring tool looks at the overall performance and gives it a rating. Whereas an analytic rubric rates a number of separate skills or aspects of a student's work, the holistic rubric looks at the "big picture" of the student's work and gives it an overall rating. The rating can be over a six-, five-, four-, or even three-level range. The holistic rubrics in this book are based on a four-level scale: "Above Goal," "At Goal," "Near Goal," and "Below Goal." Student work at the "At Goal" level represents the high standards sought.

References

Generally, many children's books on these topics could be substituted for the titles listed here.

Skeletons

Balestrino, P. (1989). *The Skeleton Inside You* (T. Kelley, Illus.) New York: HarperCollins.

Barner, B. (1996). *Dem Bones.* New York: Scholastic.

Belov Gross, R. (1978). *A Book About Your Skeleton* (S. Bjorkman, Illus.). New York: Scholastic.

Cameron, J., Maizels, D., Rosewarne, G., & Temperton, J., Illus. (1995). *The Visual Dictionary Of The Skeleton.* London: Dorlking Kindersley.

Clemesha, D., & Zimmerman, C. (1991). *Rattle Your Bones.* New York: Scholastic.

Hall, K. (1991). *Skeletons! Skeletons!* (P. Billin-Frye, Illus.). New York: Platt and Mun.

Simon, S. (1998). *Bones.* New York: Morrow Junior Books.

Wood, L. (2001). *Skeletons.* New York: Scholastic.

Solar System

Cole, J., & Degen, B. (1990). *The Magic School Bus Lost In The Solar System.* New York: Scholastic.

Fowler, A. (1992). *The Sun's Family Of Planets.* Chicago: Children's Press.

McCracken, M. J., & McCracken, R. A. (1993). *Planets In Our Solar System* (E. Peters, Illus.). Surrey, B.C., Canada: McCracken Educational Services.

Sweeney, J. (1998). *Me And My Place In Space* (A. Cable, Illus.). Dragonfly Books.

Dinosaurs

Nonfiction
Aliki. (1981). *Digging Up Dinosaurs.* New York: Thomas J. Cromwell Junior Books.

Aliki. (1985). *Dinosaurs Are Different.* New York: Harper & Row.

Asimov, I. (1920). *Did Comets Kill The Dinosaurs?* Milwaukee, WI: Fareth Stevens.

Barlowe, D., & Barlowe, S., Illus. (1977). *Dinosaurs: A Pop-Up Book.* New York: Random House.

Benton, M. (1995). *How Do We Know Dinosaurs Existed?* Austin, TX: Raintree Steck-Vaughn.

Diamond, J. (1984). *Dinosaurs.* England. Hamish Hamilton Children's Books.

Dixon, D. (2000). *Amazing dinosaurs.* Honesdale, Penn, Boydsmill Press.

Johnson, J. (1995). *Dinosaur Skeletons And Other Prehistoric Animals* (E. Gray & S. Kirk, Illus.). London: Marshalls Editions Development.

Keller, E. (1997). *Dinosaur Fun Facts.* Austin, TX: Steck-Vaughn.

Marvin, F., Illus. (1986). *How Big Is A Brachiosaurus.* New York: Platt and Munk.

Moseley, K. (1986). *The Flight Of The Pterosaurs: A Pop-Up Book.* New York: Simon & Schuster.

Most, B. (1987). *Dinosaur Cousins?* Orlando, FL: Harcourt Brace.

Most, B. (1989). *The Littlest Dinosaurs.* New York: Harcourt Brace.

Most, B. (1991). *A Dinosaur Named After Me.* New York: Harcourt & Brace.

Most, B. (1994). *How Big Were The Dinosaurs?* Olando, FL: Harcourt Brace.

Recht Penner, L. (1991). *Dinosaur Babies* (P. Barrett, Illus.). New York: Random House.

Rowe, E. *Giant Dinosaurs* (M. Smith, Illus.). New York: Scholastic.
Fiction
Bryan Cauley, L. (1988). *The Trouble With Tyrannosaurus Rex.* Orlando, FL: Harcourt Brace Jovanovich.

Duncan Edwards, P., & Cole, H. (1997). *Dinorella.* New York: Scholastic.

Keller, E. (1997). *Dinosaur Show And Tell* (J. Gieg, Illus.). Austin, TX: Steck-Vaughn Company.

Most, B. (1978). *If The Dinosaurs Came Back.* New York: Voyager Books.

6

Teaching and Assessing Reading Comprehension through the Use of Graphic Organizers

Topics in This Chapter

- ♦ Strategies for using graphic organizers to help students process information according to the thinking-skill verb used in the task.
- ♦ Strategies to create performance tasks that use graphic organizers and oral presentation.
- ♦ Strategies to create assessment tools to assess the quality of student's use of graphic organizers.

Graphic Organizers

A graphic organizer is a diagram that represents a relationship directed by a thinking-skill verb. The verb **"sequence"** calls for a diagram of a series of boxes connected by arrows that shows the "event" of one box leading to the "event" of another box. The sequence could be the events in the story. The verb **"compare"** could be supported by a diagram with two side-by-side boxes. The characteristics of one thing would be listed in one box and the characteristics of the other thing would be listed in the second box. There are many types graphic organizers that could be used to help the student organize information to make a comparison.

The purpose of a graphic organizer is to give the student support in processing information according to the thinking-skill verb in the performance task. When the student sees that the task calls for sequencing, describing, inferring, predicting, comparing, or rating, the student should eventually be able to process information on his own without the help of a graphic organizer. But while students are gaining experience in processing information, the graphic organizer is a guide.

Figure 6.1 presents the sequence of events in using graphic organizers. Notice that the sequence is in the form of a cycle. Steps A through F constitute a cycle of identifying the thinking-skill verb, getting a graphic organizer to use, using the graphic organizer to process information, assessing the quality of the work, reflecting on strengths and needs, planning for improvement, and then starting the cycle over again.

Figure 6.1 also shows a second sequence represented by steps 1 to 3. This sequence represents the work teachers do over several years, i.e., grades K–5, to coach students to be independent learners making decisions about selecting, creating, and using graphic organizers to support their thinking.

In the beginning, graphic organizers are given to the students by the teacher. Later in schooling, students select which graphic organizer to use from a wall poster. Still later, students create and use their own graphic organizers.

Figure 6.1. Using Graphic Organizers to Support Thinking

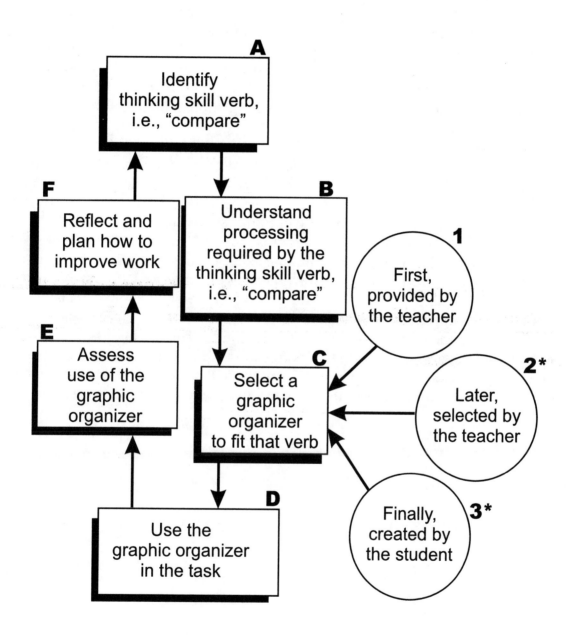

Note: These actions may not be taken by students until later in elementary school.

The Connection between Thinking-Skill Verbs, Drawings, and Graphic Organizers

The previous two chapters ask students to draw pictures and then give oral explanations of what the pictures showed. These strategies are particularly important when students are not yet ready to provide written explanations.

Drawings ask students to arrange information "on the space" of the paper. Sequences of activities are drawn in sequence. A drawing of two characters, or a character and the student side-by-side, provides the opportunity for the student to compare and contrast. The visual organization of information supports the thinking skill important to the task.

A graphic organizer is another way to organize information "in space" to support a thinking skill. Where the drawing used no written language, the graphic organizer requires the student to arrange words and simple phrases in the space of the graphic organizer. The physical act of putting the words or phrases in space supports the "pattern of thinking" required by the task.

Figure 6.2 shows a graphic organizer that supports the thinking skill of sequencing. Figure 6.3 supports the thinking skill of comparing. In both Figures 6.2 and 6.3, the student is asked to draw pictures and then add words, phrases, or sentences depending on their writing skills. These tasks show a transition from drawing to written language.

Figures 6.4 and 6.5 ask for only written responses. The thinking-skill verb in Figure 6.4 is "sequence," and the thinking-skill verb in Figure 6.5 is "explain." The teacher decides how drawing and writing will be used in a graphic organizer based on writing skills of the students and the requirements of the task.

Figure 6.2. Graphic Organizer Supporting the Thinking-Skill Verb, "Sequence"

What did the wolf do first?

First

What did the wolf do next?

Next

GO1

Figure 6.3. Graphic Organizer Supporting
the Thinking-Skill Verb, "Compare"

How are the desert and where I live different?

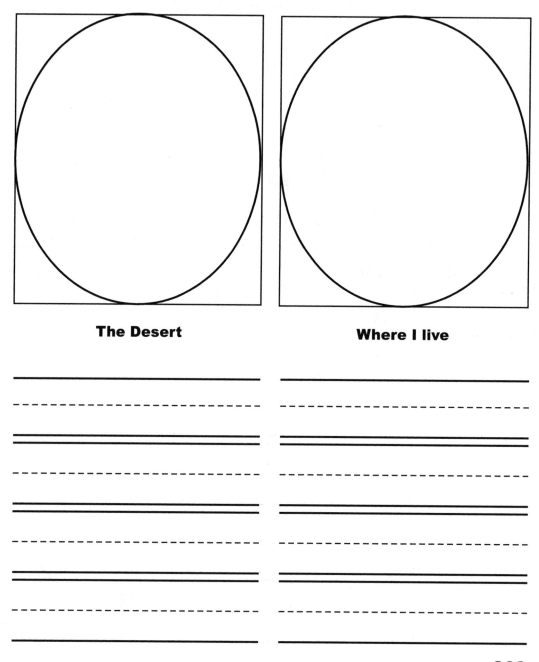

The Desert   **Where I live**

GO2

Figure 6.4. Graphic Organizer Supporting the Thinking-Skill Verb, "Sequence"

What did the wolf do when he came to the straw house?

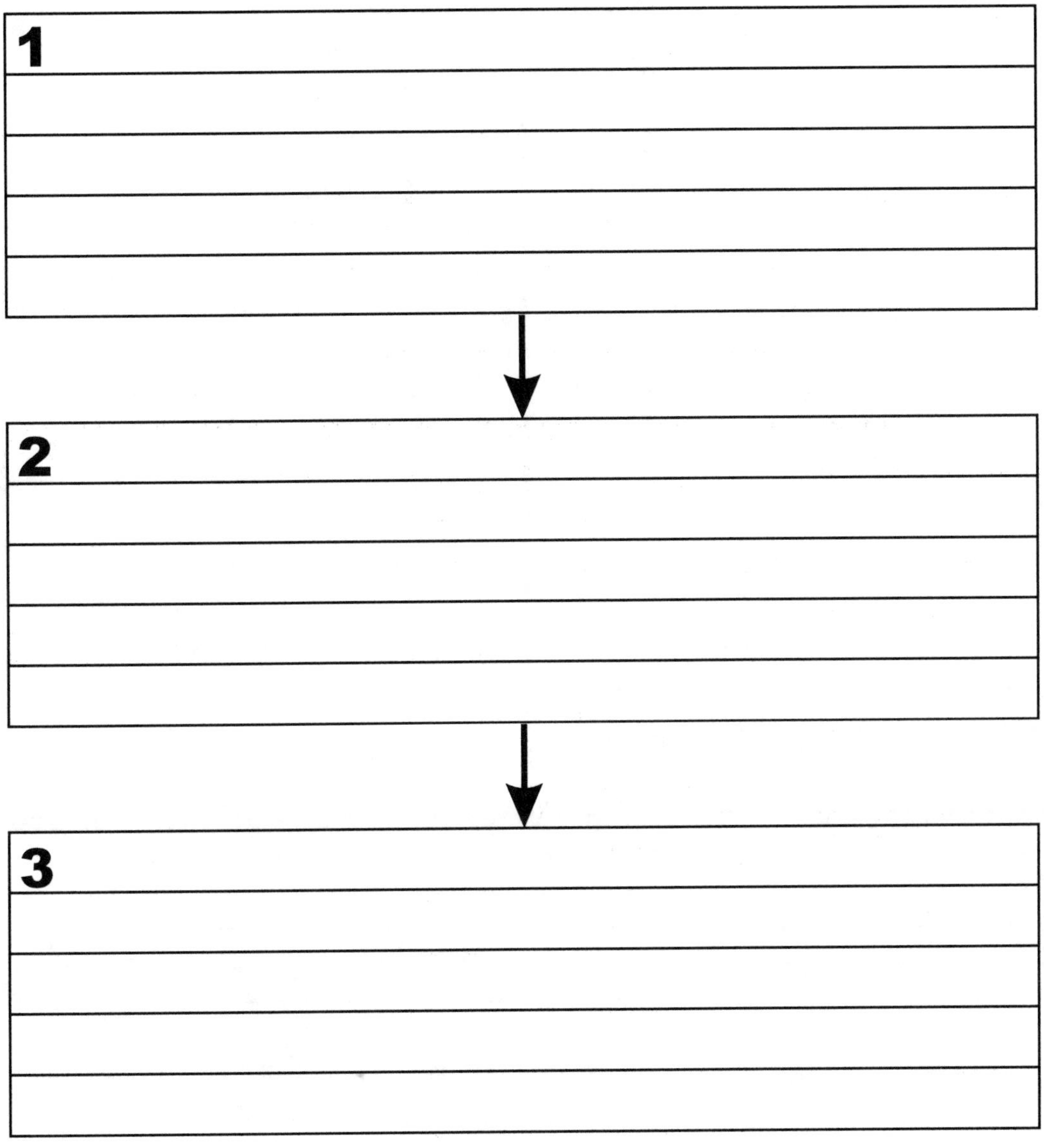

1

2

3

GO3

Note: This graphic organizer would be used only when students are ready to write.

Figure 6.5. Graphic Organizer Supporting the Thinking-Skill Verb, "Describe"

Describe what you find in a hot desert.

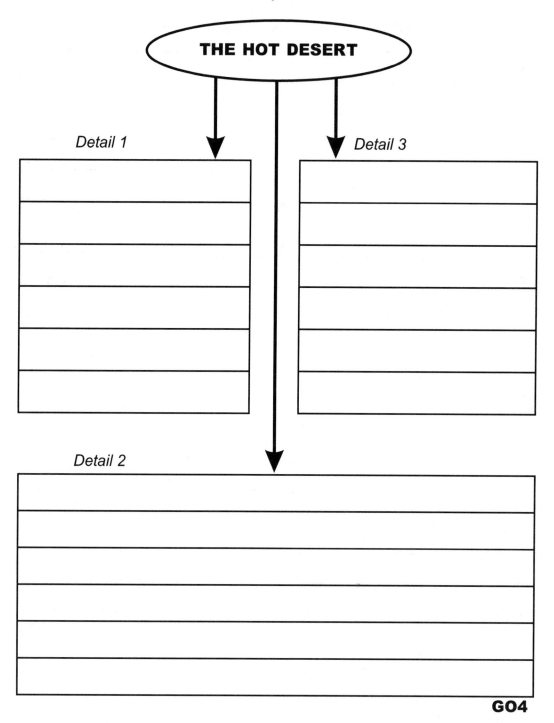

GO4

Name: _____

Date: _____

Sequencing

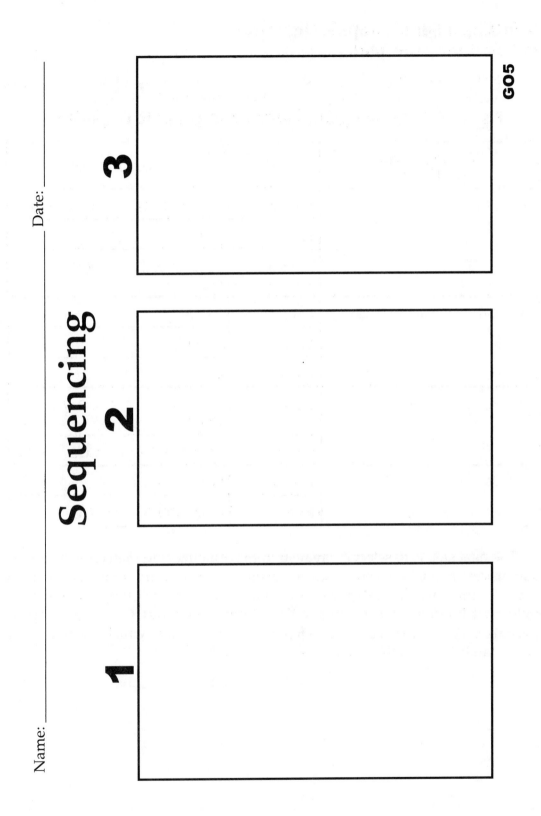

1

2

3

GO5

Selecting a Set of Graphic Organizers to Use during the Year

Select the thinking-skill verbs on which to focus during the year. A sample set of verbs selected by a first grade teacher is presented in Figure 6.6.

Figure 6.6. Thinking-Skill Verbs and Graphic Organizers

Thinking-Skill Verb Category	Verbs	Graphic Organizer(s)
Initial Understanding	Describe	GO4, GO9, GO10, GO14, GO16
	List	GO15
	Sequence	GO1, GO3, GO5, GO6, GO7, GO8
Developing an Interpretation	Categorize	GO13
	Infer	GO11
	Predict	GO13
Making Connections	Compare	GO2, GO17, GO18, GO19, GO20, GO21
	Contrast	GO2, GO18, GO19, GO20, GO22
Critical Stance	Evaluate	GO23, GO24, GO27
	Rate	GO24, GO25, GO28, GO29

The next step is to select or create graphic organizers to match the information processing that the verbs require. Twenty-eight graphic organizers are presented in this chapter. Each graphic organizer has a unique title and a reference code in the bottom, left-hand corner. For example, the code GO1 means Graphic Organizer #1. Figure 6.6 uses the references codes to show which graphic organizers can be used with which thinking-skill verbs.

Name: _____ Date: _____

First, Then, Next, Last

First

```
┌─────────────────────────────────────────┐
│                                           │
│                                           │
│                                           │
│                                           │
└─────────────────────────────────────────┘
                    │
                    ▼
```

Then

```
┌─────────────────────────────────────────┐
│                                           │
│                                           │
│                                           │
│                                           │
└─────────────────────────────────────────┘
                    │
                    ▼
```

Next

```
┌─────────────────────────────────────────┐
│                                           │
│                                           │
│                                           │
│                                           │
└─────────────────────────────────────────┘
                    │
                    ▼
```

Last

```
┌─────────────────────────────────────────┐
│                                           │
│                                           │
│                                           │
│                                           │
└─────────────────────────────────────────┘
```

GO6

Name: _____ Date: _____

Book Title: _____

Beginning, Middle, and Ending

Beginning

Middle

Ending

GO7

Name: _____ Date: _____

Topic: _____

Pie Organizer

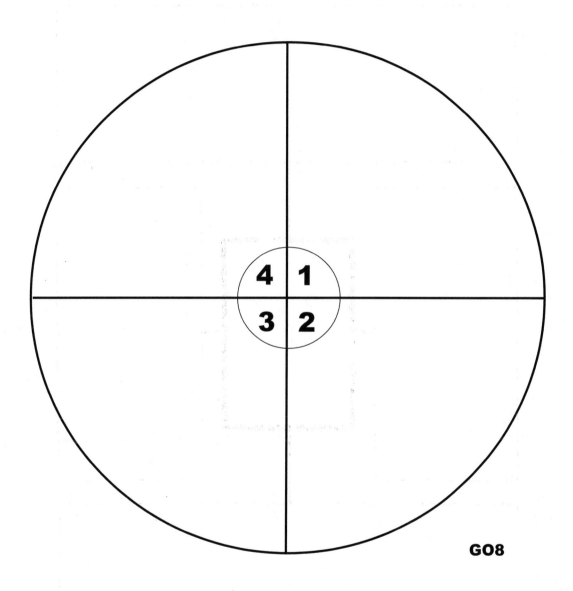

GO8

Name: _____ Date: _____

Topic: _____

Four Boxes of Details

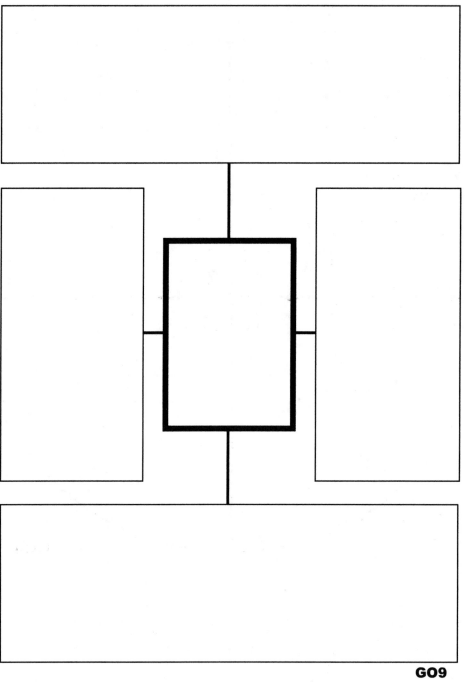

GO9

Name: _____ Date: _____

Word Splash

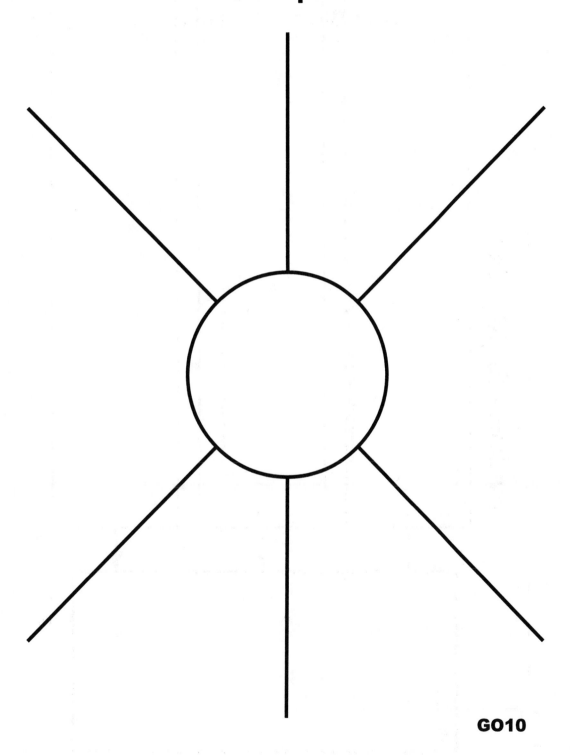

GO10

Name: _____

Date: _____

Evidence for My Idea

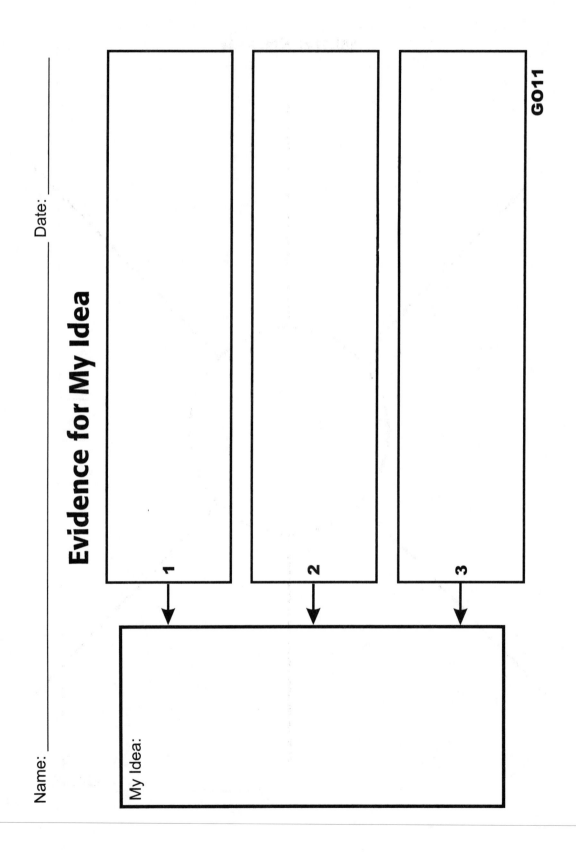

1

2

3

My Idea:

GO11

Name: _____

Date: _____

Organizing Into Two Categories

Category 1: _____

Category 2: _____

GO12

Name: _____

Date: _____

Make A Prediction

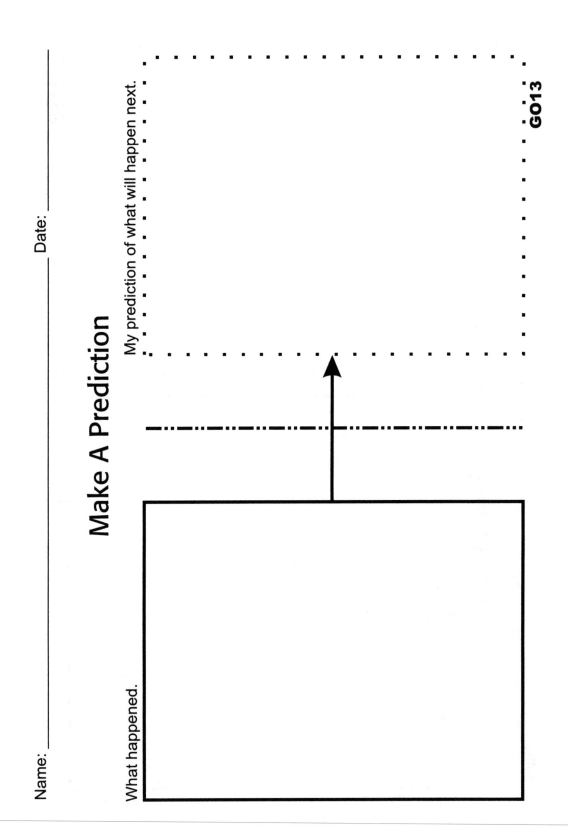

My prediction of what will happen next.

What happened.

GO13

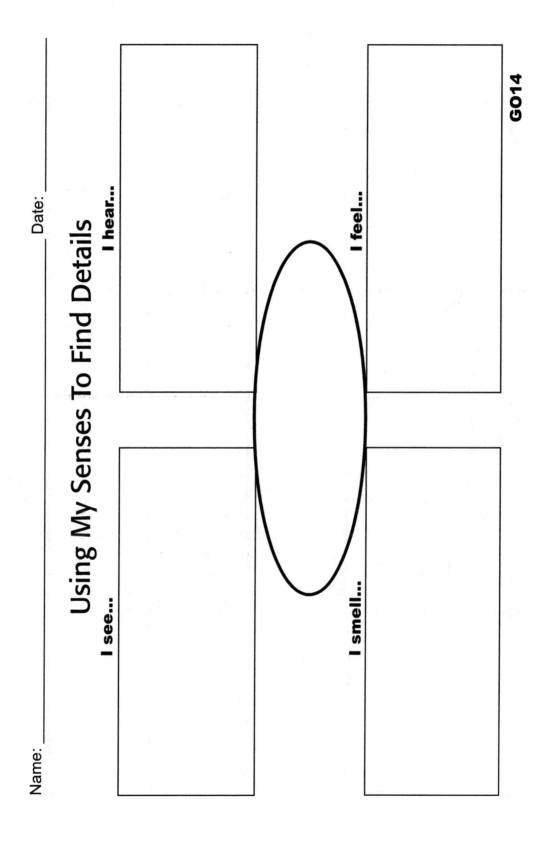

Name: _____

Date: _____

Using My Senses To Find Details

I see...

I hear...

I smell...

I feel...

GO14

Name: _____

Date: _____

Three Facts About:

1.

2.

3.

GO15

Name: _____

Date: _____

Who, When, and Where?

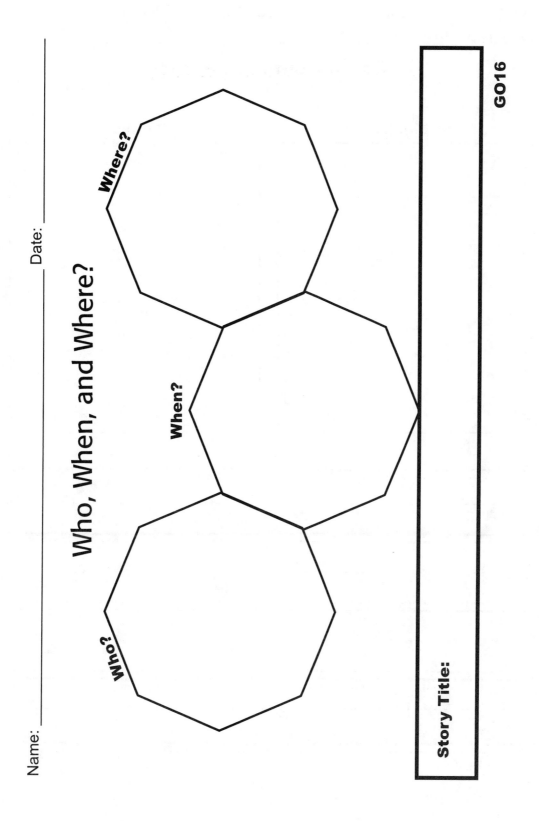

Where?

When?

Who?

Story Title:

GO16

Name: _____ Date: _____

Book Title: _____

Reality Versus Fantasy

Reality

Fantasy

GO17

Name: _____   Date: _____

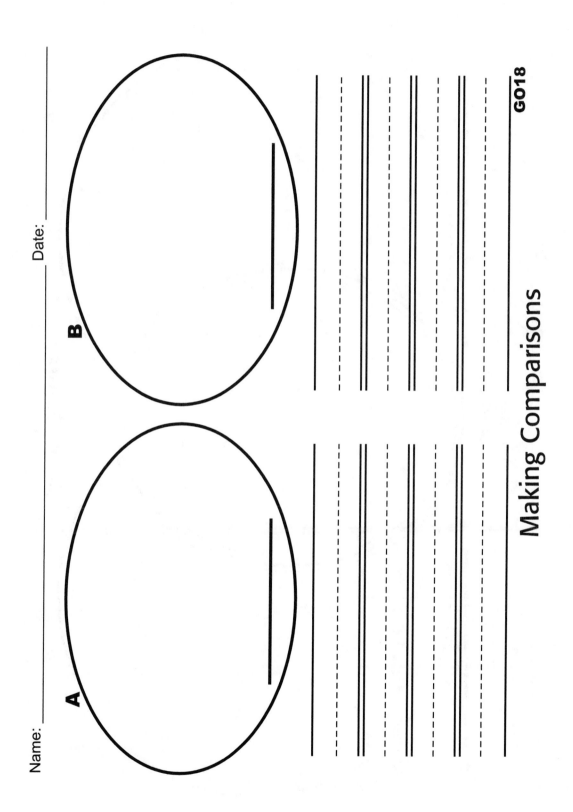

Making Comparisons

GO18

Name: _____

Date: _____

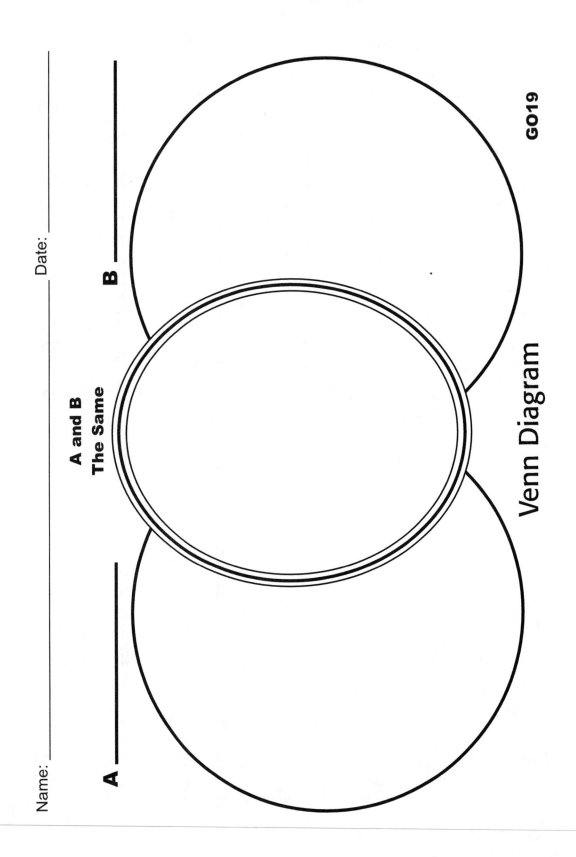

A

A and B
The Same

B

Venn Diagram

GO19

Name: _____

Date: _____

Drawings To Show Similarities And Differences

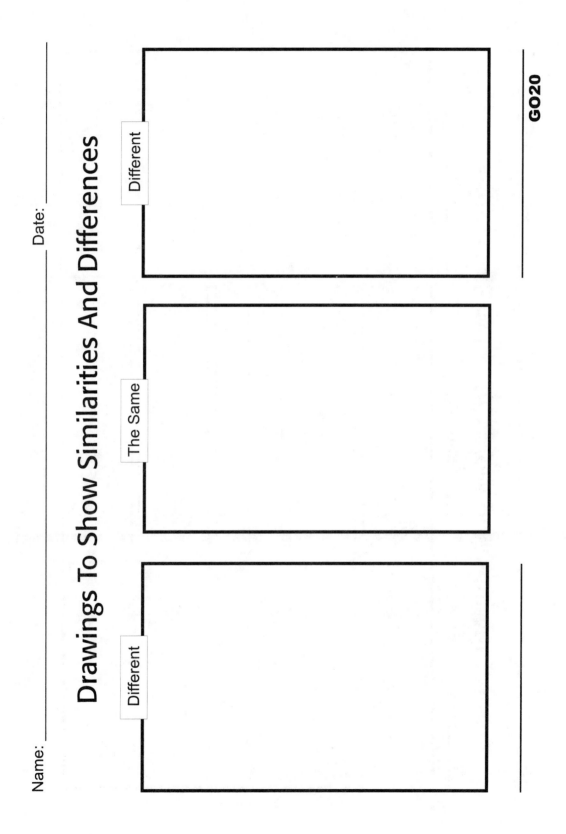

Different

The Same

Different

GO20

Name: _____

Date: _____

Drawings And Words To Show Similarities

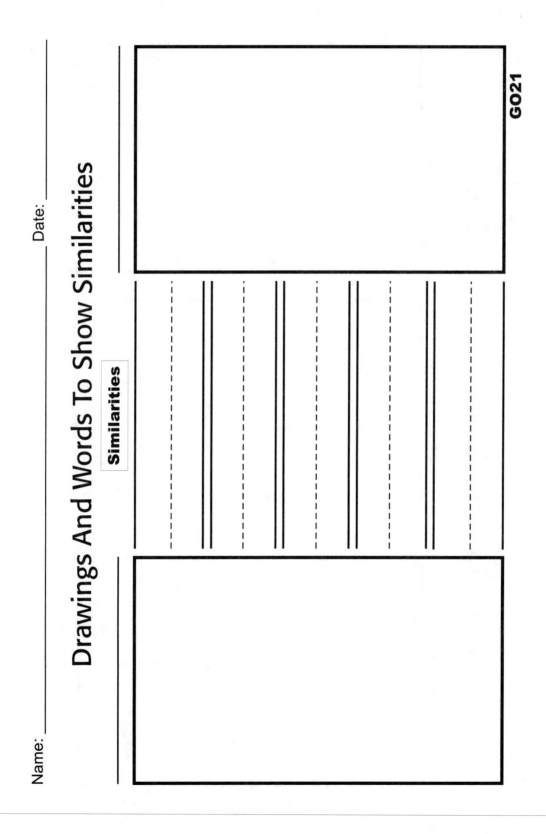

Similarities

GO21

Drawings And Words To Show Differences

Name: _____

Date: _____

Differences

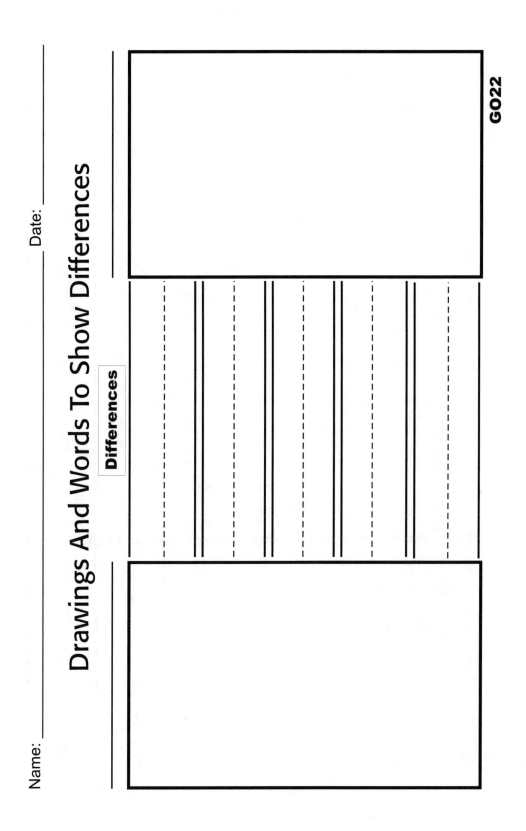

GO22

Name: _____

Date: _____

Story Title: _____

The Most Interesting Part Of The Story

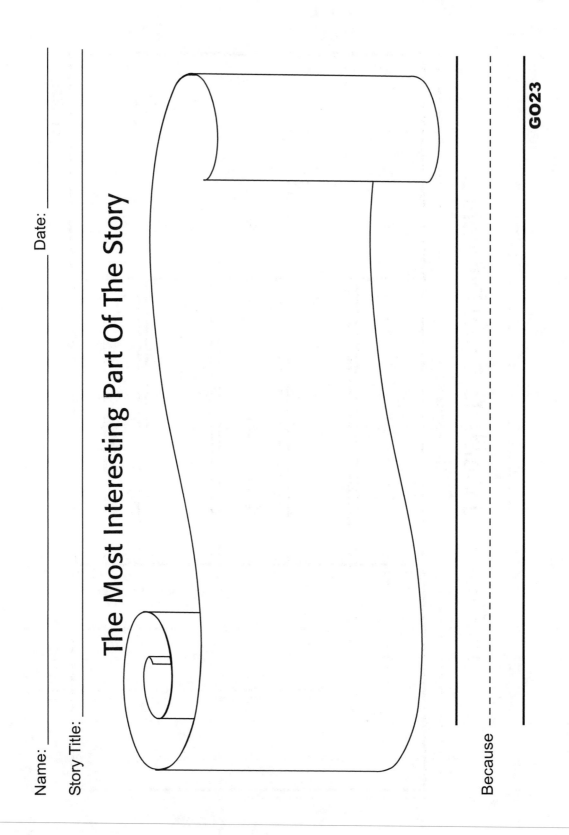

Because ------

GO23

Name: _____ Date: _____

Illustration Rating

I would rate the illustrations in _____

Terrific   OK   Needs Work

My two reasons are:

1. _____

_____

_____

_____

2. _____

_____

_____

GO24

Name: _____ Date: _____

Title Rating

Is this a good title? _____

Yes

No

And this is why I think so!

_____

- -

===

- -

===

- -

===

- -

_____

An idea for a new title is:

_____

- -

_____

GO25

Name: _____   Date: _____

Book Title: _____

Review By A Critic

Terrific	**Okay**	**Needs Work**
I think that the book is very entertaining.	I think that the book is somewhat entertaining.	I don't think that the book is very entertaining at all.

My reasons are:

_____

- -

_____
_____

- -

_____
_____

- -

_____
_____

GO26

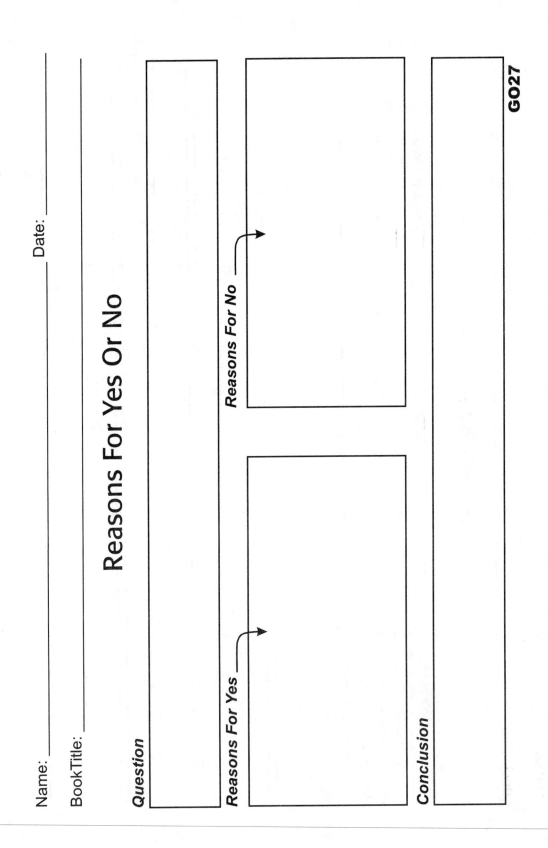

Name: _____

Date: _____

BookTitle: _____

Reasons For Yes Or No

Question

Reasons For Yes

Reasons For No

Conclusion

GO27

Name: _____   Date: _____

BookTitle: _____

Reader's Rating For Fiction

0　　　　**1**　　　　**2**　　　　**3**

I did not like　　I liked this　　I liked this　　This is my
this book at all　book a little.　book a lot　favorite book.

I liked (or didn't like) this book because

_____

- -

_____

- -

_____

- -

_____

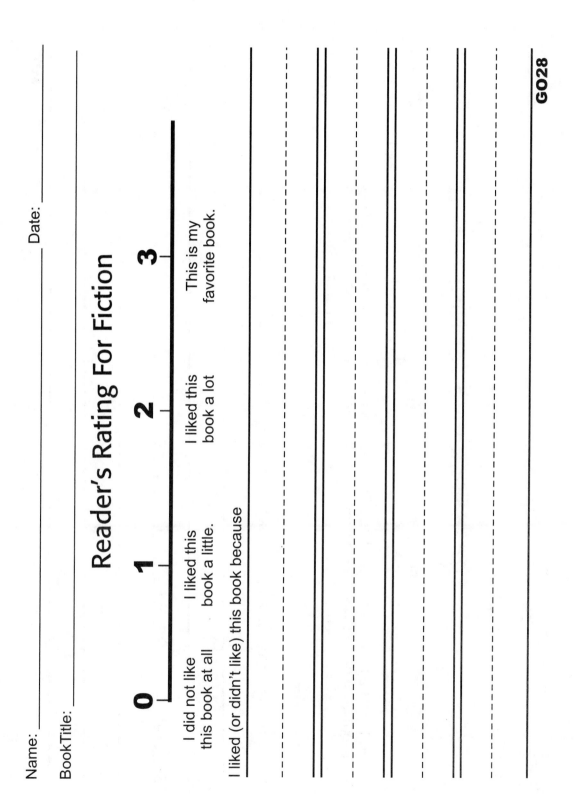

GO28

Name: _____

BookTitle: _____

Date: _____

Reader's Rating For Non-Fiction

0   **1**   **2**   **3**

This book had no information on _____

This book had some information on _____

This book had good information on _____

This was the very best book to learn about _____

This book was (was not) a good book to learn about _____

_____

because _____

_____

_____

GO29

Teaching the Students to Use Graphic Organizers

Each time a new graphic organizer is introduced to the students the teacher follows the five steps in Figure 6.7.

A. Introduce the Graphic Organizer

Explain the task to be done such as sequencing an event, showing characteristics of a thing, or comparing two things. The graphic organizer helps us do the job.

B. Teach the Students to Use That Graphic Organizer

Model the use of the graphic organizer for the students. Place information into the graphic organizer and talk about the information as you add it. The teacher may also make obvious mistakes in putting information into the graphic organizer and then ask the students to help find and correct them.

C. Provide Opportunities for the Students to Use the Graphic Organizer

♦ Whole Class

Next the teacher may work with the class in using the same graphic organizer for a new task. The teacher adds some information and asks students to come up to the easel to contribute to the graphic organizer.

♦ Pairs or Small Groups

Then the teacher may assign the task of using that same graphic organizer for a new task to a pair of students or a small group. For example, if the students as a group have learned to use a graphic organizer to show the characteristics of the desert, the small group would use that same graphic organizer to work on a new task such as to show the characteristics of cacti.

♦ Individuals

Finally, when the teacher feels that the students have enough large and small group experience with that graphic organizer, individual performance tasks requiring the use of that graphic organizer are used. Now, individual students are completing their own graphic organizers of other plants and animals in the desert.

D. Guide the Students' Self-Assessment

The teacher models using an assessment list to assess work done in a graphic organizer during the teacher's original modeling. The same assessment list is used for the small group work and then for the individual work. These assessment lists contain only two or three items.

E. Guide the Students' Self-Reflection and Goal Setting

At the end of a whole-group activity with the graphic organizer, the teacher asks, "How did we do? Terrific? Okay? Or Needs Work?" When a student volunteers a response, he or she is asked to explain. Then, the class talks about how to improve when using graphic organizers. The teacher talks to the pairs or small groups and engages them in the same assessment and goal setting. Finally, the teacher talks with individual students to discuss their self-assessment and plans to improve their individual work.

Encourage Students through Showing Off Their Terrific Work

When a student does terrific work, ask him or her to show it off and then post it for a day in the classroom. Look for opportunities to acknowledge the terrific work of students who usually do not do terrific work. Refrain from using praise such as, "You are an excellent artist." Rephrase your comments to be an encouragement by saying, "I like the way you have shown the details of how Authur looked in your graphic organizer." Praise focuses on the student and encouragement focuses on the work. Ultimately, encouragement is much more motivating to the student.

Continue the Cycle Each Time a New Graphic Organizer Is Introduced

Repeat the five steps each time a new graphic organizer is introduced. Add samples of student work to the Gallery of Excellence for each of the new graphic organizers. By the end of the year, two or three samples of student work will model the whole collection of graphic organizers learned that year.

Late in the year when the gallery presents several types of graphic organizers, the teacher may hold a whole-class meeting to discuss a new task such as sequencing the events in a new story or comparing animals from two different regions of the United States. As part of that discussion, the teacher may ask the students to suggest a type of graphic organizer to use for a specific task. Thus, the students are learning to be more independent in using graphic organizers. Ultimately, in the upper grades, students will be selecting and creating their own graphic organizers to help them in their projects.

Ask the Students to Help Select the Graphic Organizer to Use

If the teacher selects five or six graphic organizes on which to focus during the year, students can become so familiar with their use that they can work with the teacher to pick a graphic organizer for a new task. The small set of graphic organizers that comprise the collection for the year can be posted in the room. Then when an opportunity arises calling for the use of a graphic organizer, the teacher can ask, "Which one of our graphic organizers should be used this time?" The teacher accepts suggestions and asks for explanations for why a specific suggestion was made. The teacher leads the group to a consensus and that graphic organizer is used.

Figure 6.7. Teaching Students to Use Graphic Organizers

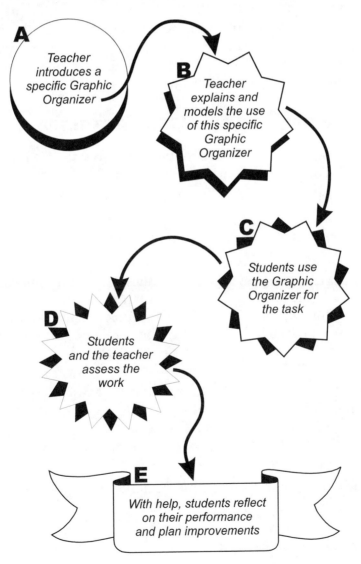

A. Teacher introduces a specific Graphic Organizer

B. Teacher explains and models the use of this specific Graphic Organizer

C. Students use the Graphic Organizer for the task

D. Students and the teacher assess the work

E. With help, students reflect on their performance and plan improvements

Analytic and Holistic Rubrics for Work Done in Graphic Organizers

As with drawing and oral presentation, analytic and holistic rubrics can be used to assess student performance in putting information into graphic organizers. Creating these rubrics also provides ideas for creating assessment lists for performance tasks. The assessment lists are the tools to help students learn to pay attention to the quality of their work and improve their performance. The assessment lists help the teacher focus on specific aspects of the student's work. The holistic rubrics allow the teacher to give an overall rating to a student's work. The analytic rubric helps the teacher identify the specific strengths and weaknesses of student work so that subsequent instruction can reinforce strengths and improve deficits.

Figures 6.8 and 6.9 present analytic rubrics for student work in graphic organizers and their oral description of their work. Each of these rubrics can be used for graphic organizers that call only for drawing and graphic organizers that ask for drawing and writing or only writing. Figures 6.10 and 6.11 present the holistic rubrics counterparts of Figures 6.8 and 6.9.

Naming the Levels of Performance

Up to and including most of this chapter, the following names are used to label the levels of quality of student performance defined by a rubric:

♦ **Terrific** refers to work that is very good for students at this grade level.

♦ **Okay** refers to work that is acceptable for students at this grade level.

♦ **Needs Work** refers to a performance that needs attention.

Another set of names for the levels of performance are introduced in this chapter and continue throughout the rest of this book (including the second volume). They are used in the holistic rubrics for graphic organizers and oral presentation of work done in graphic organizers in this chapter and they are as follows:

♦ **Extending** refers to work by students that are at the highest developmental level for the students at this grade level. In the case of this chapter, an Extending student is one who is very good at putting information into a graphic organizer as compared to most students at this grade level.

♦ **Consolidating** refers to work by students who are continuing to make progress.

♦ **Developing** refers to work by students who have moved beyond the beginning stages of this work.

♦ **Beginning** refers to work by students who are just beginning or beginning to learn to do this work such as put information into graphic organizers.

The names Extending, Consolidating, Developing, and Beginning are intended to define changes in the student along a developmental continuum.

The job of the teacher is to determine where the student is along this continuum and then to adjust instruction and materials to coach the student to grow to the next level. Temporary, flexible small groups of students at the same developmental level regarding some type of work, such as putting information into a graphic organizer, can be formed to address the common needs of those students.

Figure 6.8. Analytic Rubrics for Work Done in a Graphic Organizer

Specific Behavior	Level of Performance		
	3. Terrific	2. Okay	1. Needs Work
Information Is on the Topic	All of the information is on the topic.	Most of the information is on the topic.	Most of the information is off the topic.
Information Is Accurate	All the information is accurate.	Most of the information is accurate. No major errors are made.	Most of the information is incorrect.
Appropriate Amount of Information Is Provided	There are enough details without overdoing it.	There are a few too many or too few details.	There are too few details or no details.
Information in the Correct Spaces	All of the information in the graphic organizer is placed correctly.	Most of the information in the graphic organizer is placed correctly.	Many mistakes are made in placing information in the graphic organizer.
Vocabulary	Vocabulary related to the topic is especially well used.	Vocabulary of the topic is well-used.	Vocabulary of the topic is not well used.
Spaces between Words	Spaces are always used between words in phrases.	Spaces are usually used between words in phrases.	Spaces are not used between words.
Spelling	All spelling is correct.	High-frequency words are spelled correctly and other words are spelled so they can be read.	Mistakes are made in high-frequency words and other words.
Neat and Presentable	The work is very neat and presentable.	The work is mostly neat and presentable.	The work is neither neat nor presentable.
Overall	Terrific	Okay	Needs Work

Figure 6.9. Analytic Rubric for an Oral Presentation of Information in a Graphic Organizer

Specific Behavior	Level of Performance		
	3. Terrific	2. Okay	1. Needs Work
Presentation Follows the Pattern of the Graphic Organizer	The student's oral presentation stays right with the pattern of the graphic organizer. For example, if the graphic organizer is about a comparison, the oral presentation makes that comparison and only that comparison.	The oral presentation sticks mostly with the purpose of the graphic organizer.	The student presents the information but not in the pattern of the graphic organizer. For example, the student may present all of the information relevant to the "comparison" but the presentation does not actually make the comparison.
Presentation Includes Accurate Details	The student presents all of the details required.	The student presents most of the details required.	The student does not present enough details.
Vocabulary	The student uses all of the vocabulary required in the lesson.	The student uses most of the vocabulary required in the lesson.	The student does not use sufficient vocabulary.
Presentation Stays on the Topic	The presentation is entirely on the topic.	The presentation is mostly on the topic.	The presentation strays off the topic.
Uses Strong, Group-Sharing Voice	The student uses a good, strong, group-sharing voice throughout the presentation.	The student uses the strong, group-sharing voice for most of the presentation.	The student does not use a strong, group-sharing voice.
Overall	Terrific	Okay	Needs Work

Figure 6.10. Holistic Rubrics for Work Done in a Graphic Organizer

Level of Performance	Description of the Level of Performance
Extending	The information meets all the criteria for "Consolidating" but it is especially well chosen. Examples and vocabulary make this work stand out.
Consolidating	The information is completely on the topic, accurate, of good quantity and in the correct place of the graphic organizer. The appropriate vocabulary is used accurately. There are spaces between words and they are spelled correctly. The work is neat and presentable.
Developing	The information is mostly on the topic, mostly accurate, of reasonable quantity and mostly in the correct place of the graphic organizer. Most of the appropriate vocabulary is used accurately. There are spaces between words and the high frequency words are spelled correctly. Other words are spelled in such a way that they can be easily read. The work is mostly neat and presentable.
Beginning	The information is inaccurate, insufficient in detail, and not always placed correctly in the graphic organizer. Vocabulary on the topic is not used. Words run together without spaces between them and many are misspelled to the extent that they are difficult to read. The work is neither neat nor presentable.

Figure 6.11. Holistic Rubrics for Work Done for the Student's Oral Presentation of Work Done in a Graphic Organizer

Level of Performance	*Description of the Level of Performance*
Extending	The presentation meets all the criteria to be "Consolidating." In addition, this presentation shows special insight into the task and presents unusually interesting details. The student does an especially good job of using enthusiasm, voice, and body language to keep the attention of the audience.
Consolidating	The presentation is entirely on the topic. The information is presented according to the pattern of the graphic organizer, i.e., a sequence, a comparison with details, or a prediction with support. The vocabulary of the topic is used correctly. The student uses a good number of details to show that he or she understands the topic. The student speaks in a good, strong group-sharing voice.
Developing	The presentation is mostly on the topic. The information is mostly presented according to the pattern of the graphic organizer, i.e., a sequence, a comparison with details, or a prediction with support. Most of the vocabulary of the topic is used correctly. The student uses too few details to show that he or she understands the topic. The student's presentation voice is not of sufficient energy for all to hear.
Beginning	The information is off topic, inaccurate, and not presented according to the "pattern" required by the graphic organizer. Vocabulary is not used and the presentation voice is of poor quality.

Creating Ideas for Performance Tasks

The first step in creating performance tasks is to generate ideas for each of the four levels of comprehension. Figure 6.12 shows ideas generated for various versions of the *Three Little Pigs*. Figures 6.13 and 6.14 shows ideas generated for the study of the Southwest desert and the New England regions of the United States.

The ideas for these performance tasks use one of the thinking-skill verbs. Performance tasks can be created that include two or more thinking-skill verbs, but those tasks would be longer. For example, such a task could begin with a sequencing activity and conclude with a predicting activity. These tasks would include two graphic organizers and two assessment lists and a "stop-and-check" point between the two parts of the performance tasks. It is good to start simple and move to more complex performance tasks when the students are ready for them. Once ideas are generated, they will be turned into performance tasks with assessment lists.

Figure 6.12. *The Three Little Pigs*

Level of Comprehension and Verb	Ideas for Performance Tasks
Initial Understanding	
Describe	**Describe** what the wolf did when he came to the first pig's house.
List	**List** the three kinds of houses the pigs built.
Sequence*	**Sequence** the order in which the wolf visited the three little pigs and their houses.
Developing an Interpretation	
Categorize	**Categorize** the three houses into "Strong Houses" and "Weak Houses."
Infer*	**Infer** a character trait of the Wolf.
Predict	(In *The Three Little Wolves and the Big Bad Pig*, read up to the point where the Pig discovers the concrete house and ask for a prediction.) **Predict** what the Pig will do next.
Making Connections	
Compare*	**Compare** the three houses built by the *Three Little Pigs* to the three houses built by the *Three Little Javelinas*.
Contrast	**Contrast** the endings of the *Three Little Pigs* and the *Three Little Wolves and the Big Bad Pig*.
Critical Stance	
Evaluate	**Evaluate** the way that Steven Kellogg drew the Wolf. Did Steven Kellogg do a good job of making the wolf look mean and scary? How did he do that?
Rate	**Rate** the three books, *The Three Little Pigs* by Steven Kellogg, *The Thee Little Wolves and the Big Bad Pig* by Eugene Trivizas and Helen Oxenbury, and *The True Story of The Three Little Pigs* by Jon Scieszka. Which was your favorite story? Why?

*These ideas for performance tasks are turned into performance tasks in this chapter.

Figure 6.13. A Study of The Southwest Region of The United States

Level of Comprehension and Verb	Ideas for Performance Tasks
Initial Understanding	
Describe	**Describe** what it would be like to be standing in the desert in the daytime. Use all of your senses.
List*	**List** the animals that live in the desert.
Sequence	**Sequence** the events of how the saguaro cactus becomes a place where other animals live.
Developing an Interpretation	
Categorize*	**Categorize** the animals that are active in the daytime and animals that are active at night.
Infer	**Infer** the hardest thing about living in a desert.
Predict	**Predict** what would happen to a cactus if you dug it up from the desert and brought it to your yard and planted it there.
Making Connections	
Compare	**Compare** the summer daytime temperature in a desert to the summer daytime temperature in New England.
Contrast*	**Contrast** a saguaro cactus to a maple tree. How are they different?
Critical Stance	
Evaluate*	(Based on the book, *A Day in the Desert*, written by first-grade students) **Evaluate** how good a job the first-grade students did of drawing pictures of the desert.
Rate	**Rate** the books you have read about the Southwest deserts. Which book gave you the best information about a desert?

These ideas for performance tasks are turned into performance tasks in this chapter.

Figure 6.14. A Study of the New England Region of the United States

Level of Comprehension and Verbs	Ideas for Performance Tasks
Initial Understanding	
Describe*	**Describe** what it would be like to be in New England in the fall. Use all of your senses.
List	**List** the kinds of trees in New England.
Sequence	**Sequence** the steps in making maple syrup.
Developing an Interpretation	
Categorize	**Categorize** New England animals into "animals that live on the land" and "animals that live in the water."
Infer	**Infer** why lighthouses are important.
Predict*	**Predict** what happens when a fisherman puts a lobster pot into the ocean.
Making Connections	
Compare	**Compare** the amount of rainfall in the Southwest desert and the amount of rainfall in New England.
Contrast	**Contrast** the kinds of animals found in the Southwest desert and the animals found in New England.
Critical Stance	
Evaluate	**Evaluate** the most beautiful photograph of a New England scene.
Rate*	**Rate** the books you have read about New England. Which book gave you the best information about New England?

These ideas for performance tasks are turned into performance tasks in this chapter.

Creating the Performance Tasks

Figure 6.15 shows performance tasks that require students to both draw pictures and put written language into graphic organizers. Figure 6.16 shows performance tasks that only require students to put written language into graphic organizers. When drawings are used as an intermediate step, the teacher checks the drawings with the students before they begin to work on the graphic organizer.

Deciding What Goes in the "Procedure" Part of the Performance Task and What Goes on the Assessment List

The "Procedure" part of the performance task presents a list of steps to take to work on and complete a performance task. Note that in the "Procedure" parts of the performance tasks in this chapter, item number one is: "Use the assessment list to know what to do." It is important that the students learn to value the assessment list because the assessment list gives them clear details about what to do in the task.

Refer to the performance task in Figure 6.17 and its assessment list in Figure 6.18. Notice that the statement of procedure asks the student to write describing words. The assessment list is more explicit and has four items regarding describing words. The assessment list asks the student to pay specific attention to describing words for seeing, hearing, smelling, and feeling.

Avoid duplicating information in the statement of "Procedure" and the assessment list. Keep the statement of "Procedure" simple—like a checklist. Craft the assessment list to focus on the details of the student's work that are most important to the task.

Figure 6.15. Drawing and Writing Placed in Graphic Organizer

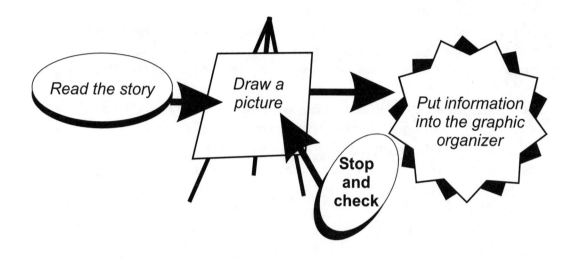

Figure 6.16. Only Writing Placed in Graphic Organizer

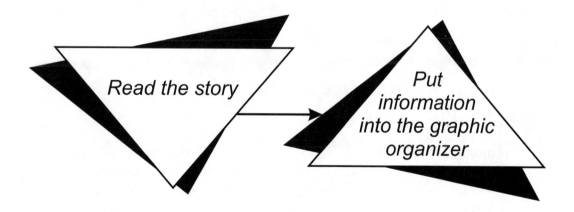

Creating Assessment Lists

All the strategies used to create assessment lists presented in the previous chapters are used here to create assessment lists that help students pay attention to the quality of their work. Assessment lists for the work done in drawings, graphic organizers that require written language, and oral presentations should be used in whole class activities, small group work, and individual work. A summary of some of the points to remember when creating assessment lists are presented here:

- Limit the number of items on the assessment list to the number of items the students can pay attention to.
- Word the items so that each is very specific.
- Attend to only one aspect of the work in any one item.
- Include "Sure Thing" items referring to aspects of the work that the students do well.
- Include one "Challenge" item to coach new learning.
- Ask the students to help create assessment lists when possible.

The assessment list also focus the teacher on specific aspects of the student's work.

The Options for the Format of Assessment Lists

The following list presents several strategies for using assessment lists during whole class, small group, and individual work.

Sentence Strip Holders

Chapter 3 showed how to create assessment lists using sentence strip holders. This format for assessment lists is well suited to whole-group activities.

Large Classroom Posters

Assessment lists for commonly used graphic organizers can be created on poster board and used repeatedly during the year when that graphic organizer is used. Used in this way, the poster version of the assessment list is well suited to whole-group work or for activities in centers.

Small Posters

Assessment lists can be created on small posters and placed in centers for activities using graphic organizers.

Assessment Lists on Paper

Assessment lists on regular paper can be used when it is desirable for the student to mark the paper to show self-assessment. The teacher then marks the assessment list to show his or her opinion of the student's work. The teacher may also write comments on the paper and use the assessment list during student conferences.

When the assessment lists are on paper, they can be sent home, saved in the student's portfolio, posted in the room or hall bulletin board, and used during parent conferences.

Performance Tasks for the *Three Little Pigs* and Regional Studies of the Southwest and New England

The following ten performance tasks have been constructed using the thinking-skill verbs and graphic organizers as final products. One task has been created for each of the ten thinking-skill verbs used in this chapter. A few use drawings as an intermediate step before the creation of a graphic organizer. When both drawings and graphic organizers are used, the performance task includes an assessment for the drawing and an assessment list for the graphic organizer. Oral presentations of the drawings and/or the graphic organizers might also be planned, but assessment lists for those oral presentations are not included here.

Coaching the Students to Use Assessment Lists Accurately

Students use the assessment list to pay attention to their work before they start, while they are working, and when they have completed the performance task. They mark the face—color it in, draw hair on it, or draw a hat on it—that shows whether they think their work is Terrific, Okay, or Needs Work. Often students are accurate in self-assessment. But when they are inaccurate, the teacher must coach them to pay more attention to the details of their work that they assessed inaccurately.

If the student has assessed their use of details as "Terrific" but the student's work is not up to that standard, the teacher asks the student to point out the details that were used. Then the teacher asks the student if there are many, some, or only a few details. Finally, the student is asked to assess whether that amount of details is at the Terrific, Okay, or Needs Work level. If the student is still inaccurate, the teacher shows the student models of student work that shows how details are used to make the work Terrific. The point is to gently coach the student to focus on the aspect of his or her work and compare it to work that is well done.

Asking Students to Help
Create the Assessment List

After the students have had experience using an assessment list with a specific type of graphic organizer, they can help in creating assessment lists for that kind of graphic organizer when it is used again. This active involvement in creating the assessment list teaches them more about paying attention to the quality of their work and improving their performance. The goal is to coach students to become more independent in their learning.

Figure 6.17a. Performance Task:
New England in the Fall

Background

You are getting ready to paint a picture in art class.

Imagine that you are standing in a field near a forest in the fall in New England. What would you see? What would you smell? What would you feel? What would you hear?

Task

Put describing words in your graphic organizer.

Audience

The audience for your describing words is your art teacher.

Purpose

These words will help you create a beautiful picture of New England in the fall.

Procedure

1. Use graphic organizer GO14.
2. Use your assessment list to see what you have to do.
3. Put the words New England Fall in the middle box of the graphic organizer.
4. Put two describing words in each box around the middle box.
5. Use your assessment list to check your work.

Figure 6.17b. Performance Task Assessment List: New England in the Fall

1. Did I put the words, New England Fall, in the middle of the graphic organizer?

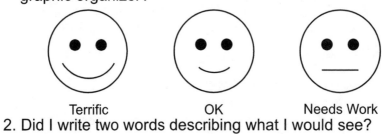

Terrific   OK   Needs Work

2. Did I write two words describing what I would see?

Terrific   OK   Needs Work

3. Did I write two words describing what I would smell?

Terrific   OK   Needs Work

4. Did I write two words describing what I would hear?

Terrific   OK   Needs Work

5. Did I write two words describing what I would feel?

Terrific   OK   Needs Work

Figure 6.18a. Performance Task: Animals of the Desert

Background
The school librarian needs a new book about desert animals. What animals live in the desert?

Task
List the animals that live in the desert.

Audience
The librarian will look at your list to see if it has four different kinds of desert animals.

Purpose
Your list can be the beginning of a classroom book about desert animals.

Procedure
1. Use graphic organizer GO15.
2. Use your assessment list to see what you have to do.
3. Put the words "Desert Animals" in the box at the top.
4. List different kinds of desert animals.
5. Use your assessment list to check your work.

Figure 6.18b. Performance Task Assessment List: Animals of the Desert

1. Did I write the words Desert Animals in the box at the top?

2. Did I write the names of four animals that live in the desert?

3. Did I choose four different kinds of animals?

4. Did I check my spelling?

Figure 6.19a. Performance Task:
The Wolf Visits The Three Pigs

Background

Pretend that you are a police detective investigating what the wolf did. What pig did the wolf visit first? What pig did the wolf visit next? What pig did the wolf visit last?

Task

Your task is to draw pictures to show the sequence of the wolf's visits to the three pigs. You will also write the words that show what each house was made of.

Audience

You will show your picture to the police captain.

Purpose

Your pictures will help the police learn about what the wolf did.

Procedure

1. Use graphic organizer GO5.
2. Use your assessment list to see what you have to do.
3. Draw the three pig houses in order.
4. Write the words that describe what each house was made of.
5. Use your assessment list to check your work.

Figure 6.19b. Performance Task Assessment List:
The Wolf Visits The Three Pigs

1. Did I draw a picture of the first pig house and write words that described what the house was made of?

Terrific   OK   Needs Work

2. Did I draw a picture of the second pig house and write words that described what the house was made of?

Terrific   OK   Needs Work

3. Did I draw a picture of the third pig house and write words that described what the house was made of?

Terrific   OK   Needs Work

4. Is my work neat and presentable?

Terrific   OK   Needs Work

Figure 6.20a. Performance Task:
Daytime and Nighttime Desert Animals

Background

Your class is working on a book about desert animals. You have already begun to make lists of animals that live in the desert. Now you will categorize those animals into daytime and nighttime animals.

Task

You will write the names of four daytime animals and four nighttime animals in the graphic organizer.

Audience

The school librarian will review your list to see if you have categorized the desert animals correctly.

Purpose

These categories will help you continue to work on your classroom book.

Procedure

1. Use graphic organizer GO12.
2. Use your assessment list to see what you have to do.
3. Put the labels "Daytime Animals" and "Nighttime Animals" above the boxes for the two categories.
4. Write the names of the animals in the correct boxes.
5. Use the assessment list to check your work.

Figure 6.20b. Performance Task Assessment List: Daytime and Nighttime Desert Animals

1. Did I write the labels Daytime Animals and Night Time Animals in the correct place on the graphic organizer?

     Terrific   OK   Needs Work

2. Did I write the names of four daytime animals in the daytime box?

     Terrific   OK   Needs Work

3. Did I write the names of four nighttime animals in the nighttime box?

     Terrific   OK   Needs Work

4. Did I check the spelling?

     Terrific   OK   Needs Work

Figure 6.21a. Performance Task:
Character Trait of the Wolf

Background

You are a newspaper reporter covering the Wolf and Pig story. What was the wolf really like? Was the wolf mean, brave, strong, creative, or friendly? You are going to write a newspaper story about the wolf and you need to think about what the wolf is really like.

Task

Select one character trait that is true about the wolf. Find evidence in the story that shows that you are correct.

Audience

The audience for your character analysis is the editor of the newspaper.

Purpose

The editor wants to know what you think about the wolf.

Procedure

1. Use graphic organizer GO11.
2. Use the assessment list to see what you have to do.
3. Complete the phrase, "The wolf was _____" in the dark box on the graphic organizer.
4. Find three pieces of evidence from the story and put them in the other boxes in the graphic organizer.
5. Use your assessment list to check your work.

Figure 6.21b. Performance Task Assessment List:
Character Trait of the Wolf

1. Did I complete the phrase, "The wolf was _____"?

2. Did I show three pieces of evidence for the character trait?

3. Did I list the page number of the book to show where I found the evidence?

4. Did I use complete sentences to show my evidence?

Figure 6.22a. Performance Task:
Lobster Pot

Background
Pretend that you are a lobster fisherman living in Maine. You go out on your lobster boat and put many lobster pots into the ocean.

The next day, you and your friend come back and pull up each lobster pot. Your friend asks you, "What do you think will be in the next lobster pot we pull up?

Task
Your task is to predict what would be in a lobster pot when you pulled it out of the ocean. You will draw a picture first. Then you will complete a graphic organizer.

Audience
Your picture and graphic organizer are for your friend.

Purpose
You are helping your friend learn what gets into lobster pots.

Procedure
1. Remember to check your assessment lists to see what to do.
2. First draw a picture on a blank piece of paper. Show what you predict would be in the lobster pot when you pull it out of the ocean.
3. Next, use graphic organizer GO13.
4. Write the phrase, "When a lobster pot is put into the ocean…" in the first box.
5. List the things that you predict will be in the lobster box in the second box.
6. Remember to use your assessment lists to check your work.

Figure 6.22b. Performance Task Assessment List: Lobster Pot (Drawing)

1. Did I draw a picture that shows what I predict will be in the lobster pot?

2. Did I use accurate details?

3. Did I use color to show what things look like?

4. Did I label the things I drew?

Figure 6.22c. Performance Task Assessment List: Lobster Pot (Graphic Organizer)

1. Did I write the phrase, "When a lobster pot is put into the ocean..." in the first box?

Terrific	OK	Needs Work

2. Did I list at least three things that could be in a lobster trap when it is pulled out of the ocean?

Terrific	OK	Needs Work

3. Is my spelling correct?

Terrific	OK	Needs Work

4. Is my work neat and presentable?

Terrific	OK	Needs Work

Figure 6.23a. Performance Task:
Pigs and Javelinas

Background
Susan Lowell wrote a version of the *Three Little Pigs* called *The Three Little Javelinas*. Jim Harris drew the pictures.
How are these two stories the same?

Task
Your task is to see if the pig houses are like the houses of the javelinas.

Audience
You will show your pictures to your parents when they come to Open House.

Purpose
Your pictures will help you tell your parents about the books you are reading.

Procedure
1. Use the assessment list to see what you have to do.
2. Use graphic organizer GO21.
3. Label one circle "pig house" and one circle "javelina house."
4. Draw pictures of the two similar houses.
5. Write a sentence describing each house.
6. Use your assessment list to check your work.

Figure 6.23b. Performance Task Assessment List: Pigs and Javelinas

1. Did I find a pig house and a javelina house that were similar?

Terrific   OK   Needs Work

2. Do my pictures show how the two houses are similar? Did I show details of both houses?

Terrific   OK   Needs Work

3. Do my labels and sentences describe how the two houses are similar?

Terrific   OK   Needs Work

4. Did I begin each sentence with a capital?

Terrific   OK   Needs Work

Figure 6.24a. Performance Task:
Saguaro Cactus Versus Maple Tree

Background

The nature center wants to create a display of how the Southwest desert plants are different from the plants found in New England.

Task

Your task is to draw pictures and complete a graphic organizer that shows how a saguaro cactus is different from a maple tree.

Audience

The audience for your work will be the people who visit the nature center.

Purpose

Your pictures and writing will teach the nature center visitors about desert and New England plants.

Procedure

1. Use the assessment lists to see what you have to do.
2. Use graphic organizer GO22.
3. Draw a picture of a saguaro cactus and a maple tree.
4. Write the differences between the cactus and the tree.
5. Make an oral presentation of how the cactus and the tree are different.
6. Use the assessment lists to check your work.

Figure 6.24b. Performance Task Assessment List: Saguaro Cactus Versus Maple Tree (Drawing)

1. Did I draw a detailed picture of a saguaro cactus?

Terrific   OK   Needs Work

2. Did I draw a detailed picture of a maple tree?

Terrific   OK   Needs Work

3. Do my pictures show the differences between the cactus and the tree?

Terrific   OK   Needs Work

4. Did I label the parts that show the biggest differences?

Terrific   OK   Needs Work

Figure 6.24c. Performance Task Assessment List: Saguaro Cactus Versus Maple Tree (Graphic Organizer)

1. Did I put the words Saguaro Cactus above one box and the words Maple Tree above the other box?

2. Did I write three differences between the cactus and the tree?

3. Did I draw a line from my writing to the parts of the picture that show those differences?

4. Is my work neat and presentable?

Figure 6.24d. Performance Task Assessment List: Saguaro Cactus Versus Maple Tree (Oral Presentation)

1. Did I explain three ways the saguaro cactus is different from the maple tree?

Terrific   OK   Needs Work

2. Did I use my large group sharing voice?

Terrific   OK   Needs Work

3. Did I ask my audience what questions they had for me?

Terrific   OK   Needs Work

4. Did I answer their questions?

Terrific   OK   Needs Work

Figure 6.25a. Performance Task:
Student Artists

Background

The first-grade students from the Robert Taylor Elementary School in Henderson, Nevada wrote and illustrated a book entitled, *A Day in the Desert*. Did those first-grade students do a good job of drawing pictures of what the desert is really like?

Task

Your task is to evaluate the drawings and decide if they are good pictures of the desert.

Audience

You will send your evaluations to Robert Taylor Elementary School.

Purpose

Your evaluations will help students and teachers at Robert Taylor Elementary School know what to do if they write more books.

Procedure

1. Use your assessment list to see what you have to do.
2. Use graphic organizer GO24.
3. Evaluate the illustrations.
4. Write an explanation of your evaluation.
5. Use the assessment list to check your work.

Figure 6.25b. Performance Task Assessment List: Student Artists

1. Did I evaluate the illustrations?

Terrific   OK   Needs Work

2. Did I write two reasons for my evaluation?

Terrific   OK   Needs Work

3. Did I use a capital letter to begin each sentence?

Terrific   OK   Needs Work

4. Did I use the proper end punctuation for each sentence?

Terrific   OK   Needs Work

Figure 6.26a. Performance Task:
Research about New England

Background

You and your classmates are doing a research project on New England. You have seen many books about New England. Some books are good for research. Some books are not so good for research.

Task

Your task is to pick a book and give it a rating.

Audience

Your rating is for your classmates who are doing research on New England.

Purpose

Your rating will help other students know which books are good for research about New England.

Procedure

1. Use the assessment list to see what you have to do.
2. Use graphic organizer GO29.
3. Rate the nonfiction.
4. Explain your rating.
5. Use the assessment list to check your work.

Figure 6.26b. Performance Task Assessment List: Research About New England

1. Did I write the name of the book on the graphic organizer?

2. Did I rate the book?

3. Did I give one good reason for the rating I gave the book?

4. Did I check my spelling?

References

Variations on *The Three Little Pigs*

Claverie, J. (1946) *The Three Little Pigs* (retold and illustrated by author). United States, North-South Books.

Kellogg, S. (1997). *The Three Little Pigs* (retold and illustrated by author). New York: William Morrow.

Lowell, S. (1992) *The Three Little Javelinas* (J. Harris, Illus.). New York: Scholastic.

Parkes, B., & Smith, J. (1984). *The Three Little Pigs* (E. Kasepuu, Illus.). London: Rigby.

Scieszka, J. (1989). *The True Story of the 3 Little Pigs* (L. Smith, Illus.). New York: Penguin Books.

Trivizas, E., & Oxenbury, H. (1994). *The Three Little Wolves and The Big Bad Pig*. New York: Scholastic.

Zemach, M. (1988). *The Three Little Pigs*. Canada: Harper Collins Canada.

Ziefert, H. (1995). *The Three Little Pigs* (L. Rader, Illus.). New York: Penguin Books.

Regional Studies of the United States: Southwest

A Day in the Desert. (1994). [Written and illustrated by first-grade students at Robert Taylor Elementary School in Henderson, Nevada]. St. Petersburg: FL:

Bash, B. (1989). *Desert Giant*. San Fransico: Little, Brown.

Benjamin, C. (1999). *Footprints in the Sand* (J. Rogers, Illus.). New York: Scholastic.

Cobb, V. (1989). *This Place is Dry* (B. Lavellee, Illus.). New York: Walker.

Gibbons, G. (1996). *Deserts* New York: Holiday House.

Lesser, C. (1997). *Storm on the Desert* (T. Rand, Illus.). New York: Harcourt Brace.

Marsh, T. J., & Ward, J. (1998). *Way Out in the Desert* (K. J. Spengler, Illus.). Flagstaff, AZ, Northland.

Nabhan, P. (2001). *Efrain of the Sonoran Desert* (original by A. Astorga; J. K. Miller, Illus.). El Paso, TX: Cinco Press.

Owings Dewey, J. (1991). *A Night and Day in the Desert*. Canada, Little, Brown.

Yolen, J. (1996). *Welcome to the Sea of Sand* (L. Regan, Illus.). New York: Scholastic.

Regional Studies of the United States: New England

Bernard, R. (1999). *A Tree For All Seasons.* Washington, DC: National Geographic Society.

Blackstone, M. (1995). *This is Maine* (pictures by J. Segal). New York: Henry Holt.

Bruchac, J. (1996). *The Maple Thanksgiving* (A. Vojtech, Illus.). Parsipany, NJ: Celebration Press.

Burns, D. (1990). *Sugaring Season* (photographs by C. Walsh Bellville). Minneapolis: Carolrhoda Books.

Giambarba, P. (2000). *Cape Cod Light* Yarmouth Port, MA: On Cape.

Gibbons, G. (1991). *Surrounded by Sea.* Boston: Little, Brown.

Good, E. W. (1990). *Fall is here! I love it!* (S. Shenk Wenger, Illus.). Intercourse, PA: Good Books.

Hopkinson, D. (1997). *Birdie's Lighthouse* (K. Bulochen Root, Illus.). New York: Aladdan Paperbacks.

Krupinski, L. (1994). *A New England Scrapbook.* New York: HarperCollins.

Lasky, K. (1983). *Sugaring Time* (photographs by C. G. Knight). New York: Macmillan.

Lobel, A. (2000). *One Lighthouse One Moon.* Singapore, China: Tien Wah Press.

London, J. (1995). *The Sugaring-off Party* (paintings by G. Pelletier). New York: Dutton Children's Books.

MacDonald, G., & Weisgard, L. (1946). *The Little Island.* New York: Scholastic.

Martin, C. E. (1984). *Island Winter.* New York: Greenwillow Books.

McCloskey, R. (1953). *One Morning in Maine.* New York: Viking Press.

McCloskey, R. (1977). *Time of Wonder.* New York: Puffin Books.

Pallotta, J., & Bolster, R. (1990). *Going Lobstering.* Watertown, MA: Charlesbridge.

Ropp, P., & Ropp, C. (1985). *Keep the Lights Burning Abbie* (pictures by P. E. Hanson). Minneapolis: First Avenue Editions.